Michigan State
Multiple Offense

Michigan State
Multiple Offense

Clarence "Biggie" Munn

Head Football Coach
Michigan State College

NEW YORK
PRENTICE-HALL, INC.
1953

Printed in the United States of America

L. C. Cat. Card No.: 53-12498

DEDICATION

This book is dedicated to all of the players with whom I have become associated in football, men with courage and faith and red-blooded enough to play in a wonderful game of physical combat.

Publisher's Foreword

During the past few years the multiple offense system of football has grown rapidly in popularity. The coach who has perhaps done more than anyone else to develop this style of exciting offensive play is Clarence "Biggie" Munn, head football coach at Michigan State College.

Coach Munn's outstanding success with the multiple offense is shown by the consistently fine competitive record of Michigan State teams under his direction. Coach Munn and his staff of assistants have continually worked hard to make additions and refinements to this system, and this book presents for the first time a comprehensive discussion of the Michigan State multiple offense.

Probably the greatest advantage of the multiple offense as developed at Michigan State has been that it incorporates the best features of various offensive formations. The varied nature of the attack makes it difficult for an opposing team to prepare an adequate defense for each offensive system used.

Then, too, the new rule in college football that curtails the use of two platoons (one for offense and one for defense) increases the effectiveness of a varied offense. It is no longer possible for a team to devote a week's practice to perfecting defenses designed to halt each formation of the multi-system attack. If the opposing team spends an excessive amount of time developing adequate defenses for the varied offenses possible, much less time will be available for perfecting its own offensive strategy.

The Michigan State multiple offense, as Coach Munn has pointed out, is well adapted to exploiting to the fullest the opposition's defensive weaknesses. The use of the various offensive formations early in a game will enable the quarterback and coach to determine which offense will be most successful against any particular opposition. By concentrating on this effective offense a team may be able to gain a great initial advantage that the opposing team will find exceedingly difficult to overcome.

Coach Munn has utilized his years of experience, both as college coach and All-American player, to present a simply written but complete account of the techniques involved in one of football's most modern and successful offensive systems

Contents

Michigan State
Multiple Offense

Introduction

Twelve of my twenty-one years of college coaching were spent as an assistant under three successful head coaches—Bernie Bierman of Minnesota, Ozzie Solem of Syracuse, and Fritz Crisler of Michigan. I have been fortunate to have coached during a period when football has made its greatest strides. It has been a great privilege to know and associate with some of the outstanding coaches of all time, men who have added so much to this wonderful game. A few of these are "Doc" Williams of Minnesota, Alonzo Stagg of Chicago, "Pop" Warner of Stanford, Andy Kerr of Colgate, Knute Rockne of Notre Dame, Lou Little of Columbia, and Fielding H. Yost of Michigan.

I feel that my association with these fine gentlemen has benefited me greatly and has increased my knowledge of football, thereby contributing a great deal to any success that I have achieved in the profession. Many of my associations in football have come from high school coaches, and I have been fortunate to have made hundreds of lasting friendships among them.

In the ensuing chapters, I am going to try to put forth my ideas of offensive football and explain the evolution of the Michigan State offense. There were quite a number of factors that brought this evolution about, and I will try to show the development from the early stages to the present. I want to emphasize that all of the methods described here are based exactly on our way of doing things at Michigan State. They may not be the very best, but they have proved sound to us in practical application to our over-all offensive scheme.

The game of football is a rugged one, and it takes a fine, high-type young man to play the game. Our country was founded on the basic principles of hard work and fair play, by men with tremendous desire and initiative. Boys who become great in football must possess these same qualities. It speaks well for our game that so many young men who have participated in football have gone on to become outstanding successes in all walks of life. I am sure they benefited by the many lessons they learned on the football field. Early in his career the successful football player learns that it takes much work and effort to become really good in any endeavor.

I have learned that it is impossible to tell a good football player by his height or his weight. The main qualities of a football player are intangible and can only be put to test in competition. I am speaking of qualities such as *heart* and *desire*.

When you get a group of boys with an abundance of these intangibles along with some physical ability, you have ideal material from a coach's standpoint. I have been fortunate during my career to have many young men of this type. To them I will always be deeply grateful for the major part they played in any success that I have achieved myself. Any coach can have a lot of plays and diagrams and the finest system in the country, but it is the team spirit and unity of the players themselves that are the deciding factors in success or failure.

I wish to acknowledge the great help my splendid staff has accorded me in the compilation of the material for this book. Thanks are due to Duffy Daugherty, line coach; Earle Edwards, end coach; and Steve Sebo, backfield coach. They have cooperated with me in the way that they have always done in the past, which only enhances my belief that I have the finest staff to be found anywhere in the coaching ranks.

We have only one sign in our dressing room at Michigan State: *"The Difference between Good and Great is a Little Extra Effort."* It has been our motto throughout the years. When a boy is imbued with this spirit and has the physical ability to go along with it, it's a tough combination to beat.

1

Evolution of the Michigan State Offense

To follow the evolution of the Michigan State offense, it is necessary for me to go back to my early coaching days. The first opportunity given to me in the coaching profession was a result of being hired by Bernie Bierman as an assistant at my alma mater, the University of Minnesota. Naturally, my ideas of offensive football were influenced greatly by this past master of the game, so when I embarked on my first head coaching job at Albright College, in 1934, I decided to use the single wing attack with an unbalanced line, as a basis for my offensive running formation. I placed great emphasis on the buck lateral series, which Bierman had used, and was still using so successfully, at the University of Minnesota.

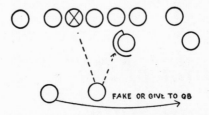

Fig. 1. Buck Lateral Series. The ball is passed to the fullback, who fakes or gives it to the quarterback.

In the buck lateral series, the ball is passed to the fullback, who carries it into the line and either fakes or gives it to the quarterback, who at the snap of the ball has pivoted around and is facing his own fullback. The purpose of this maneuver is to hold the defensive men, particularly the linebackers, in position long enough for the offensive men to gain blocking angles.

Offensive football today is a game of movement and blocking angles. Movement necessarily deals with personnel, which I shall discuss later. Blocking angles are achieved through offensive formations and techniques.

My first two years as a head coach at Albright College taught me a lot of valuable lessons. My offensive repertoire consisted primarily of the buck lateral series and direct hits by either the fullback or tailback, and a couple of half-to-half reverses.

In 1936, I spent one year as an assistant coach at Syracuse under Ozzie Solem, and then followed eight years as an assistant under Fritz Crisler at the University of Michigan. In 1946 I ventured out again as a head coach, this time at Syracuse University.

My basic conception of offensive football had expanded to include not only the buck lateral series, the direct hits by the fullback and left halfback, and the half-to-half reverses, but also the spinner series of single wing football, originated by Dick Harlow, former coach at Harvard University, and used very successfully by Crisler at Michigan. I also used a smattering of "T" formation plays, which were primarily quick hand-offs and pitch-outs.

In the spinner series the ball is passed to the fullback and he fakes or gives it to either the tail or wingback, faking to one and giving to the other—or he fakes to both and keeps the ball himself, with the play usually accompanied by a trap block at the line.

So, at this time our offense had progressed to the

point where we came out of the huddle and lined up in an unbalanced "T," occasionally running a dive or pitch-out, but more often shifting to a single wing with the right halfback in the various positions seen in Figure 3 and 4. I want to point out that we always ran from an unbalanced line. This factor enabled us to

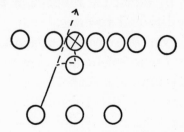

Fig. 2. Unbalanced "T" Formation.

keep our blocking assignments constant while operating from many backfield formations.

In 1947, after having accepted the head coaching job at Michigan State and finding our personnel not adapted to the conventional single wing attack, we had to make some changes in our ideas of offensive football.

Fig. 3. Unbalanced Single Wing, Wing-back Up.

I would like to state here and now that our present Michigan State offense evolved to its present level mainly for two reasons: first, the various offensive maneuvers, techniques, and formations were added together to get the maximum use out of the personnel at hand; and second, these offensive methods were used as countermovements because teams had successfully halted our existing formations by placing their defensive alignment so that it stopped the strongest parts of our offense.

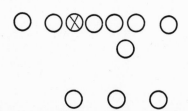

Fig. 4.   Unbalanced Single Wing, Wingback Deep.

At Michigan State, in 1947, we had halfbacks who were good runners but not adept in the use of the forward pass.   It so happened that our quarterback was a better than average passer, so we began to throw more from the "T" formation, using an unbalanced line. The strongest point of the unbalanced "T" is its ability to hit the short-side flank very quickly.   To get the maximum use out of our passing attack in the "T," we placed the right halfback up as a wingback, which gave us a winged "T" formation.

9

Our opponents began to "defense us" by using a balanced or an undershifted defense against our "T," figuring correctly that we were much stronger to the short side than we were to the strong side. Against our single wing formation they would overshift their defensive personnel to stop our number-one strength on the strong side. These defenses are diagrammed in Figures 5 and 6.

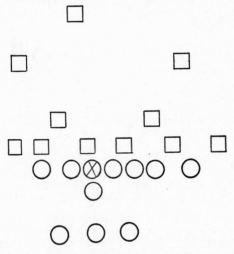

Fig. 5.   Defense Lineup vs. "T" Formation.

Through the latter part of the 1947 season these defensive maneuvers began to cause us great concern because they were handicapping a good execution of our offense. As a staff, we began to think about how we could prevent our opponents from defensing our

"T" as a strictly passing and a short-sided formation, and of how we could take advantage of the defenses that we would meet invariably in a game.

It took us until the early part of the 1948 season to work out an attack that could successfully cope with this problem. By experimenting in practice

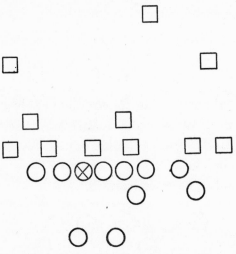

Fig. 6.   Defense Lineup vs. Single Wing Formation.

against various types of defenses, we found that we could retain practically all of our blocking principles and, with very few changes in assignments, could pass the ball from our "T" formation or from our winged "T" through the legs of our quarterback directly to the fullback, enabling us to run our buck lateral and spinner series without shifting to the single wing.

This immediately created another problem for the opponent's defense, which is what we are always trying to do from an offensive standpoint. Now our opposition had to defense our "T" and winged "T" forma-

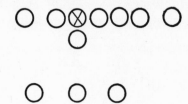

Fig. 7. "T" Formation.

tions not only as passing formations but they also had to try to stop the offensive maneuvers that followed.

First of all we would come out of the huddle and line up either in a "T" or a winged "T" formation as diagrammed in Figures 7 and 8.

Fig. 8. Winged "T" Formation.

We would either run quick-hitting "T" plays with the quarterback handling the ball; pass with the quarterback doing the passing; pass the ball through the quarterback's legs and execute a spinner or buck lateral play, hitting at any point along the line; or shift to the single wing formation with the right halfback possibly being in an up or deep position. From the very beginning, this maneuver, what we call our *"T" single wing* formation, was a great success and has helped our offense probably more than any other single formation. I believe this is primarily because we pass more from this formation than any other, which naturally makes it a very effective running formation.

Fig. 9. "T" Double Wing Formation.

Throughout the 1948 and 1949 season, we kept adding plays to our existing formations and tried to perfect the various techniques. In the spring of 1950, we began experimenting with a "T" double wing formation, which is diagrammed in Figure 9.

We started out by feeling that here we finally had one of the finest passing formations in the history of football, and, to our knowledge it was not being used by any other team in the nation. The deep double wing as originated by Glen S. ("Pop") Warner, and exploited so successfully by Andy Kerr of Colgate, had

13

been a very good passing formation, so we figured that we could accomplish the same purpose from the "T" double wing, which would give us four deep receivers and create an added problem for the pass defenses.

We opened the season in the fall of 1950 with this formation and scored a touchdown with a pass on the second play. It wasn't long, however, before teams started forming automatic defenses whenever we came out of the huddle in the "T" double wing formation. Invariably they would set their defenses to stop what they figured would be a pass, so it turned out eventually that we were doing more running than passing from this formation. This change was successful because of the simplicity of our offensive numbering system (which will be explained in Chapter 2), and the fact that our blocking principles were readily adaptable in this "T" double wing.

At this point we had at our disposal the following formations: The unbalanced "T," the winged "T," the single wing with the deep wing back, and the single wing with the up wing. Throughout the remainder of the 1950 season and all through 1951 we tried to use the type of attack best suited to our personnel. For example, when I would use a starting backfield of McAuliffe, Pisano, Panin, and Dorow, we were more apt to use a power attack to utilize the power running of these backs. And when I had a pony backfield on the field consisting of Yewcic, Bolden, Slonac, and

Wells, it often suited our purposes to utilize some of our fast-hitting "T" offenses. At times during these years we would shift into left formation, but we had primarily an unbalanced line to the right.

In the spring of 1952 we decided that it might be just as effective to use the left halfback as a flanker on the short side, with the rest of our personnel in an unbalanced "T" alignment as diagrammed in Figure 10. It gave us a lot of additional pass patterns on the short side and a double-team block, if necessary, on the de-

Fig. 10. "T" Formation with Left Half Up.

fensive tackle. This formation was used quite effectively throughout the 1952 season.

It is true that none of these formations would be very effective if they lacked the proper personnel to block, pass, and to carry the ball. However, we feel strongly that with the variety of our multiple offense, we can best utilize the qualities that a certain offensive *individual* might possess.

In this chapter I have tried to give the reasons for adopting the type of offense that we are now using.

In the ensuing chapters, as the numbering system and the techniques and principles involved in our offensive scheme are explained in detail, I hope to give a complete and clear picture of what we are trying to do at Michigan State from an offensive standpoint.

2

Simplified Numbering System

We feel that our numbering system is very simple and, at the same time, flexible and effective. It is adaptable for use on any level of football, starting with junior high and progressing through high school, junior college, and college. I have used this numbering system in post-season all-star games when few practices were available. The *simplicity* of our signal system enabled me to give a great deal of instruction in offense to the squads and to have them master the maneuvers in the short time available.

There are many different numbering systems being used in football today. One of the most popular is the numbering of defensive holes. In 1932, 1933, and 1934, Bernie Bierman numbered offensive seams, and the success that his teams achieved speaks highly for his system. At Albright College, Syracuse, and Michigan there was a great deal of thought and planning given to a system by which we could number the offensive men. We tried to devise a signal system that could operate on offensive blocking principles, enabling us to give our plays requiring a single assignment for each offensive man regardless of the defensive alignment of our opponents. We tried this system at the University of Michigan and it proved to be very successful. At Michigan State we have made numerous revisions and have added to it during the past six years.

How the numbering system works

Our numbering system consists of two zones and seven numbered offensive men. Everything hitting at the strong-side flank outside of our offensive end is the 1-zone. Our strong-side end is our No. 2 man; our strong-side tackle is the No. 3 man; our outside guard, the No. 4 man; inside guard, the No. 5 man; center, No. 6 man; the short-side tackle, No. 7 man; short-side end, the No. 8 man; and everything outside of the short-side end is the 9-zone.

Fig. 11. Offensive Numbering.

I don't like to call these line positions "right" or "left." By referring to them as either *short side* or *strong side,* we can shift into a left formation and always have the same offensive alignment. In other words, our strong-side end, who would be our *right* end on the *right* formation, would also be our strong-side end or our *left* end if we went into *left* formation. This holds true all the way along the line and enables us to run our entire offense from a left formation without any additional blocking assignments. The only change would be that, from right formation, the linemen pull or block in the opposite direction.

Fig. 12. Left Formation Numbering.

The last digit of any signal given in our system tells where the ball is going to be run. In other words, for any signal ending in "1," the play will end up at the strong-side flank. When any signal is called ending with the number of one of our offensive linemen, it means that the play will go over him and that he will have a key block on the play.

For example, we might hit over a single man using a half-dozen different techniques in the backfield, but the fact that his number was the last digit of the signal would immediately tell him the play was eventually going to hit over him and that he would have a key block to perform.

This system enables us to have our blockers operate by principles that, with very few exceptions, are workable against any and all types of defenses. For example, if a play is called over one of our offensive linemen and he has the key or the *lead block,* as we call it, we don't tell him to block a defensive guard or a defensive tackle, and so on. We tell him to block the first man in at the hole or the first man out at the hole. Our offensive blockers try to have good blocking angles as often as possible.

In our indirect attacks, such as the spinner and buck lateral series, when one of our lead blockers has a man on him, we have a principle whereby he pulls and his post blocker automatically becomes the lead. We tell our offensive linemen that there are only two positions a defensive man in their territory can have. The opponent is playing either "on" him or "off" him, so the lead blocker has the very simple principle of pulling away from the play when there is a man on him and lead blocking when he is free.

The actual techniques that we use in the execution of these fundamental blocks, such as the lead post block I have just mentioned, will be discussed in the chapter on offensive line play.

In a great number of our plays, when we have a lead post block going in one direction, we will have what we term an *inside-out block* going in the opposite direction, the lead post block being the power block and the inside-out block being more of a position block.

This inside-out technique is commonly referred to as a *mousetrap block,* but we like the "inside-out" terminology because this defines specifically what we want our man to do when executing this type of block. We tell him to pull and hit for the tail of the hole man and block from the inside out. We always attempt to open holes laterally rather than by driving the defensive men backwards. We try to follow a set of blocking principles not only at the line, but in our blocks on linebackers and in our downfield blocking as well.

In describing the development of our offense, I started with our basic single wing formations. In giving you our signal system, I will start on that basis, giving you the signal series used in our single wing attack, and then attempt to show the flexibility of our numbering system and the way we were able to correlate the variety of offensive formations to this same principle of numbering offensive men.

We have divided all of our single wing plays into two categories. For any play numbered from zero through 99, we have our right halfback in a deep position. This "zero formation" is shown in Figure 34 in Chapter 5.

When the right halfback assumes a position as an upwing or a flanker, it automatically becomes a 100-type formation. In a "22" play, for example, the halfback is in a deep position, but if he were to move to an up position, the play would be called "122."

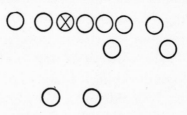

Fig. 13. "100" Formation.

We have divided our offense into different series. We do not number the backfield men. The signal series is presented to the boys in this manner: zero to 10 are plays where the ball is passed to the fullback and he hits directly at any point along the line.

In the 10 to 20 series, the ball will go to the fullback and he will either give the ball to the wingback on a reverse or will fake to him, keeping the ball and carrying into the line. On this spin series, the fullback naturally always spins toward his wingback.

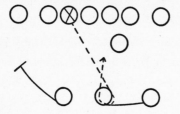

Fig. 14. 10 to 20 Series. Ball to fullback, who fakes or gives to wingback.

On the 20 to 30 series, the ball goes to the fullback. He always spins toward the tailback and will fake or give to the tail or the wingback.

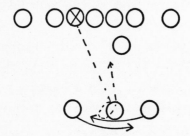

Fig. 15. 20 to 30 Series. Ball goes to fullback, who fakes or gives to tailback or wingback.

For example, on a "21" or "22" play, he would give to the tailback; on the "23," "24," and "25" play he would fake to the tailback, sometimes fake to the wingback, and keep on a complete spinner hitting into the line. On a "27," "28," and "29" he would fake to the tailback, give to the wingback, and continue his fake into the line.

On the 30 to 40 series, the ball goes directly to the tailback and he hits direct anywhere along the line. On the 40 to 50, which is the buck lateral series, the

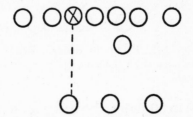

Fig. 16.   30 to 40 Series.   Ball goes to
tailback, who hits direct.

ball goes to the fullback and he will fake or give the ball to the quarterback.

For example, on a "41" play the fullback will carry the ball in and give to the quarterback, who in turn will lateral to the tailback. On a "44" play the fullback will carry the ball in and fake the ball to the quarter-

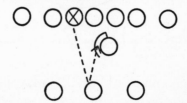

Fig. 17.   40 to 50 Series.   Ball goes
to fullback, who fakes or gives to
quarterback.

back; the fullback will keep it and continue on into the line with the short-side tackle trapping out at the hole over the No. 4 man.

I mentioned before that we have two single wing formations. We can run all of our single wing plays from both of these formations and the only man affected is the wingback. In other words, if we call a "44" play, he would be in a deep position, and if we called a "144" play, he would be in an up position.

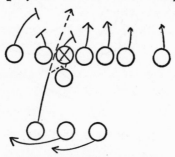

Fig. 18.   Left Half at 7.

When we started running a few plays from the "T" formation, our first thought was to correlate the signals as much as possible with our single-wing numbering because we wanted to retain the basic principles involved in our signal system. We decided finally that any time the quarterback handled the ball directly from the center, we would call that play by naming the back who would eventually end up carrying the ball and also name the offensive man or zone over which he would hit.

In other words, a straight dive by the left halfback with the quarterback handing him the ball and having him hit over our No. 7 man, we number "left half at 7." When we have the quarterback handing to the left halfback on a flank play, hitting the strong-side flank, we call that "left half at 1."

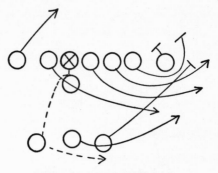

Fig. 19. Left Half at 1.

To carry this thinking further, we decided that as long as we called our single wing formation with our wingback up our *100 formation,* it would simplify things to call our winged "T" formation our *"T" 100 formation.* In other words, if a quarterback wanted to dive the left halfback over our No. 7 man from the straight "T," he would simply call "left half at 7" on the starting count, which would usually be "Ready hike." If he wanted to run the same play with the right halfback up as a wingback, after finding out that the opposition changed their defense for this formation, he would simply say " 'T' 100 left half at 7," using the same starting count.

When we decided to start passing the ball from our "T" and our "T" 100 formations (passing through the quarterback's legs directly to the fullback), we

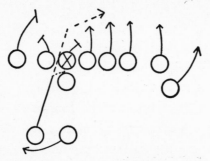

Fig. 20.   "T" 100, Left Half at 7.

found that once again the simplicity of our numbering enabled us to use the same signals by simply prefacing them with the letter "T."

Thus, if we ran our spinner trap play from the single wing, it would be called a "24" or a "124" play,

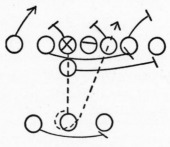

Fig. 21. "T" 24.

depending on the position of the wingback; the same play could be run without changing a single assignment by passing the ball through the quarterback's legs to the fullback and having him execute his spin from that position, calling it a " 'T' 24 play."

This method holds true for any play from our single wing that originates with the ball being passed directly to our fullback, and, as you may have gathered from our different single wing series, this constitutes the major portion of our single wing offense.

When we run from the "T" double wing, our quarterback simply names the formation, the back who will end up carrying the ball and the offensive man that he will hit over. Therefore, if we are going to buck the fullback with a hand-off from the quarterback in our "T" double wing formation, it would be called "double wing, fullback at 4," "double wing, fullback at 5," and so on, depending on the spot where we wanted our fullback to hit. If we wanted to sweep the flank with either half, we would call "double wing, left half at 1" or "double wing, right half at 9."

As this signal system begins to unfold, you can now see the tremendous possibilities of hitting over each offensive man with a wide variety of ball-handling in the backfield. Many different techniques may be used while still retaining the same blocking principles at the line.

The last formation added to our offense also

adapted itself very well to our signal system. When we want the left halfback to move up and be a wing-back on the short side, we designate that before call-

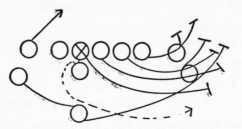

Fig. 22. "T" Double Wing, Left Half at 1.

ing the play. This usually will have no effect on the assignments of the other ten men.

In other words, if we wanted to sweep the short side with the left halfback being used as a wingback

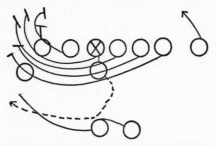

Fig. 23. Left Half Up, Right Half at 9.

on that side, we would call the play "left half up, right half at 9." If we wanted to dive the fullback over our 7 man from this formation, we would call it "left half up, fullback at 7."

29

In a later chapter I will take one offensive lineman and show the many different plays that can be run over him with fundamentally the same blocking at the line. This will be covered thoroughly in the description of our team running offense.

Theory of numbering pass plays

By this time you may be wondering why I haven't mentioned any numbers for pass plays. In our passing attack, we deviated from the method of calling passes by numbers. We have found it more suitable to name the passing technique that we are going to use and then simply describe the path of the primary receiver and the man the pass is designed to set free. If we are going to pass from our "T" 100 formation, we would simply say " 'T' 100 pass" and then describe the pattern that we want to execute—for example, " 'T' 100 pass, left end cross," " 'T' 100 pass, right end in and away," and so on.

The minute a pattern is called the other potential receivers immediately know the lanes they are supposed to run in their endeavor to clear the area for the number one receiver—and they must always be prepared to catch the pass themselves. If we are going to pass from the single wing with the fullback getting the ball, spinning and giving to the left halfback, with the left halfback dropping back to throw, we would call "spin pass, left end cross," "spin pass, left half flat," "spin pass, right end in and away," "spin pass, right half flat," and so on.

If we are going to pass from the buck lateral series with the fullback carrying the ball into the quarterback and having him drop back and throw from the single wing formation we would call "buck lateral pass, left end cross"; "buck lateral pass, right end out." Here again, as in our running attack, we can throw the same pass patterns with many different techniques and maneuvers.

All of our passes that are associated directly with the running play are called by the same number as that run with the designation "pass" at the end of it—for example, "41 pass," "29 reverse pass," "fake, right half at 6 pass."

We want to impress upon our boys that the success of these passes depends on their looking exactly like the running play. We also occasionally will put in special passes for individual games and will give them special names. Such examples would be a "Notre Dame sideline pass," an "Ohio State flanker pass," or any others with designations not included in our system.

The actual description of our pass patterns and what we are trying to accomplish with our passing attack will be treated in Chapter 7 on team passing offense.

We don't claim that our signal system is the best. There are many fine football teams throughout the country using entirely different methods of calling their plays. However, we *do* feel that our method is best suited to the type of offense we are using. Occasionally we find instances where our blocking principles are not as workable as we would like to have them be, but we are working constantly to eliminate these flaws and are naturally attempting to come closer to perfection.

The huddle, shift, and starting count

Our huddle has been devised to enable our quarterback to get the play and the starting signal to the other ten men without any confusion. Each man is in a position where he can see the quarterback's lips and hear his voice distinctly, so that there can be no misunderstanding of the signals. At the same time, we want to keep the defensive team from hearing the plays that are given in our huddle.

We have our center, or No. 6 man, spot the huddle six yards back and one yard to the right of the ball. He faces away from the ball toward his own goal. Directly on his left, facing the same direction, is our strong-side tackle, or No. 3 man. Our No. 2 man, or strong-side end, stands to left of the No. 3 man and faces away from the ball. To the right of our center and facing the same direction we have our short-side tackle, or No. 7 man, and standing at right angles to him is our short-side end, or No. 8 man. The fullback, left halfback, and right halfback take their respective positions, which face the 2, 3, 6, and 7 men at a distance approximately seven yards from the line of scrimmage.

All of the men forming the outside perimeter of our huddle stand in an erect position. Our two

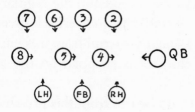

Fig. 24. The Huddle. Arrows point
in the direction players are facing.

guards, the No. 4 and No. 5 men, stand with their hands on their knees in the opening directly in front of the three backfield men, and they both face the open end of the huddle.

The quarterback remains outside of the huddle until he has made a definite choice of play. When he has arrived at a decision, he will walk into the opening of the huddle and give the play, the starting count, and the command, "Break." This arrangement may be seen in Figure 24.

Upon the command "Break," the 2, 3, 6, 7, and 8

men start directly for their positions in the line of scrimmage. The 4 and 5 men swing to the right of center, and the quarterback, fullback, and two halfbacks follow the line up in their respective pre-shift formation, which is usually an unbalanced "T" or a winged "T" formation, described previously as our "T" 100 formation.

The center puts both hands on the ball immediately. The remaining linemen have their hands on their knees and do not assume the regular three point offensive stance until the quarterback gives the signal, "Set." (Occasionally we run from this hands on knees position and the ball is snapped on the command of "Set.")

If the ball is to be run from this pre-shift formation and the linemen have assumed their set position, the starting signal is "Ready hike." There is no pause between the "ready" and the "hike." If a single wing play has been called, our backs and ends will shift on the command of "ready hike" to their respective single wing positions. This shifting is done on a "1-2-3" count with each man stepping first with the foot that is nearer the direction he is shifting. In other words, the right halfback shifting from his "T" position to a single wing back position would step right on "1" step with the left foot on "2," and set both feet on the third count.

These operations will be described in greater detail in a later chapter on backfield play. We have tried to achieve the same cadence in our single wing starting count as in our shift, using 1-2-3-4, and so on, with a smooth rhythm.

3

Offensive Line Play

In teaching line play at Michigan State, we have to take many things into consideration. It is important to have a basic set of fundamental principles that will enable our linemen to do an effective job of blocking in our various formations. During the past few seasons when we exploited the free-substitution rule to the fullest extent, we found that the so-called "guard-type" boys, weighing approximately 185 to 200 pounds, with a lot of speed and agility, were the best suited for our type of attack. Because of rule changes affecting free substitution we have had to find boys who can do the offensive job that we require and, in addition, perform equally well on defense.

Stance and take-off

In offensive line play everything naturally starts with the stance. We give our players considerable leeway in the type of stance they may use, and no two will use exactly the same. We permit them to use a square stance with their feet on the same plane, or a slight drag-like stance with one leg back of the other. We do, however, require them to follow certain fundamentals in arriving at an offensive stance. Their "tails" should be up with their backs on a horizontal plane so that they may move out in any direction. Their feet should not be any wider apart than about the width of their shoulders. There should be little or no weight on their hands.

Our offense is predicated on a fast take-off. Consequently, all of our drills in group work are designed to improve the take-off and reaction time of our linemen. Every offensive drill used is done with our team starting count.

Blocking practice

Our daily practice sessions last for about an hour-and-a-half, and for half of this time the linemen will be in group work with the line coach working on the necessary techniques to make our blocking sharp and our power offense successful.

We have found that it is not advisable to spend too much time on any one drill, so the type of drill is usually changed at intervals of 7 or 8 minutes. Good linemen become great only through constant repetition of a few types of blocks thousands of times until they develop an automatic explosiveness.

Types of blocks

I would like to list the types of blocks that go into our so-called "indirect attack." I am now referring to our spinner and buck lateral series, whether run from the single wing or the "T" single wing. After the following list I will describe each one, giving you the principles we follow in teaching them to our linemen:

1. Lead post block
2. Inside-out block
3. Check block
4. Outside-in block

5. Blocks on linebackers
6. Pass protection blocks
7. Downfield blocking

Lead post block. In discussing our numbering system I explained that our lead blocker always had an angle on the man he was to block. The lead blocker uses a step block, in which he always steps with the foot nearest the man receiving his block, aiming where the defensive man *will be* and not where he is before the play starts. The defensive man should be hit at the upper thighs or the waist with the full breadth of the blocker's shoulders. He starts driving up through the defensive man's chest immediately, bringing his outside leg up and around to prevent the defensive man from sliding into the path of the ball carrier. The blocker takes him laterally rather than from straight back.

In conjunction with our lead block, the post block is used. Our post blocker has only two functions: first, he breaks the charge of the defensive man; and second, he keeps the seam closed between himself and his lead blocker. He executes the latter by taking a short step toward his lead blocker with the foot nearest the lead blocker. He does not charge out at the defensive man. He has to remain strong and not allow himself to be forced back very far, because we invariably have an inside-out block coming from the opposite direction.

This combination, or tandem, lead post block is one of the most effective in football. We feel that any two average offensive men should be able to handle the very toughest defensive man when this technique is used properly.

Inside-out block. Most of the time when we are using a lead post block we will have an inside-out block coming from the opposite direction. Years ago, this type of block came to be known as a "mousetrap" and was predicated pretty much on allowing the defensive lineman to cross the line of scrimmage unmolested and then blocking him from the side. In modern football, where defensive linemen are not penetrating when there is no pressure on them, it becomes increasingly difficult to get an inside position on them.

We teach our linemen to execute an inside-out block by pulling and stepping with the foot in the direction they are going. They get their depth on the first step and start right up into the hole on the next step, thus getting an inside position on the defensive man where they hit him at the upper thighs or the waist with a high shoulder block. With the forearm brought in as a hook to provide additional blocking surface, they drive up through the defensive man's chest, bringing the outside leg around to prevent him from sliding into the path of the ball carrier.

We are trying to do just what the term suggests— block from the *inside out.* We assume that the defensive lineman is not going to charge and that our lineman must run up inside to get a good blocking position on him. If the defensive man *does* penetrate, it is very simple for a heads-up lineman to alter his course and use a reverse shoulder or reverse body block, following the principle of always keeping his head between the man he is blocking and the path of the ball carrier.

Check block.   In making a check block at the line, we use two different techniques.   If the defensive man's charging is consistently strong, we teach our linemen to use a high shoulder block.   Our player steps into the defensive man with the near foot, making contact first and then getting position on the second step; he places his body between the defensive lineman and the path of the ball carrier.

The second of our two techniques is used if the defensive lineman is hitting and sliding.   Here, we go out at him, hook his near knee, and crab block on all fours.   We try to pin him at the line of scrimmage to prevent him from sliding to the play.   We shoot the near arm and shoulder by the defensive lineman's thigh and hook his knee.   The offensive lineman hooks the knee of the defensive lineman with his own leg and crab blocks on all fours.

Outside-in block.   One of the most difficult blocks to execute in football is what we call an "outside-in" block.   An example would be the pulling out of a guard and his attempt to block a defensive end.   To be successful, this maneuver calls for some good acting on the part of the offensive linemen.

In teaching this type of block, we have our linemen start out as if they were executing an inside-out block, in which they move up inside of the defensive man and actually invite him to the inside to fight the pressure. Once the defensive man steps forward to meet this pressure from the inside, the blocker immediately throws his head to the outside of the defensive man, using a cross body block in an attempt to hook the defensive man inside from the outside.

Blocks on linebackers. We use two types of blocks on linebackers. In the case where we already have a good blocking angle, we send the offensive man directly at the linebacker and have him use a high block, always keeping his head between the linebacker whom he is blocking and the path of the ball carrier. We call this a *driving block on linebacker.*

Whenever the offensive man assigned to block a linebacker does not have a blocking angle and he is depending on a backfield maneuver to freeze, or hold in place, the defensive linebacker long enough for him to get a good blocking position, he executes a position block on the linebacker by running to a point where he can place his body between the defensive linebacker and the path of the ball carrier, making it necessary for the linebacker to get by him if he is to successfully make the tackle.

Pass protection blocks. Our pass protection will

vary according to the type of passes we are throwing. If our quarterback or left halfback is throwing the dropback type of pass with no run involved, we form a cup, blocking tackle on tackle, guard on guard, and use the center as a free blocker to help out wherever he is needed. We use two backfield men to block the defensive ends.

In this type of pass protection we give our offensive men an option. If the defensive man is coming in hard consistently, we allow the offensive man to break his charge by stepping into him with a hard shoulder block and then chucking back, always keeping a wide base and using a high shoulder block to prevent the defensive man from getting to the passer.

We want our offensive linemen to move their feet laterally and always to keep between the defensive man and the passer. If the defensive man is varying his charge and type of line play, we don't like to have an offensive man go out at him. We prefer to let the defensive man react and then try to keep between the defensive man and the passer, using the same high shoulder block with a good wide base.

On a running pass, we try to block just as near to a run as we possibly can. The lineman takes the normal blocking distance he is allowed on a pass play and tries to hook the defensive man by using a check block as he would in a run. We want our pulling linemen to be good actors and make it look like a running play; however, they should not go past the line of scrimmage.

A third type of pass protection is used on a jump pass. On this type of pass two offensive linemen pair off and kick out at the defensive linemen who are trying to break the jump passer's charge, thus enabling him to come right up to the line of scrimmage before throwing the ball. In order to be successful, we must get the defensive linebackers to react and expect a run—then we jump pass over their heads.

Now that I have described six of the blocks that we endeavor to teach our linemen, I want to diagram one of our plays. This is a trap play on a defensive guard, and we call the method of blocking used here our *four technique*. It is usually the first play that I will give out to any squad because it shows better than any other single play that I can think of, the dif-

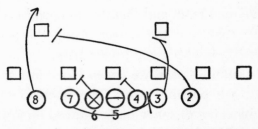

Fig. 25. Four Technique. 2—driving block on linebacker; 3—position block on linebacker; 4—lead block; 5—post block; 6—check block; 7—inside-out block; 8—downfield block.

ferent blocking techniques that are used in our offense. In the chapter on our running offense, I will show you how this one particular play can be run with a wide variety of backfield maneuvers, but right now I would like to diagram the line blocking to illustrate the execution of the types of blocking I have already described.

Pulling and downfield blocking

We work a lot on downfield blocking, because we know that it is the key to springing backs loose for the long touchdown runs.   As a staff, all of us are constantly striving to make our boys conscious of getting downfield in front of the ball carrier and making the little extra push that will send him all the way for a touchdown.

Techniques.   To get pulling linemen downfield in a hurry, it is necessary to have a good, sound method of drawing them out of the line and "around the Horn." We have found that the step-out method of pulling best fills our offensive needs.   In pulling, we have our lineman step toward the direction in which he is going so that he gets just enough depth to clear the next offensive lineman; he shifts all of his weight over the leg he is stepping with.   The angle of the second step will depend on whether he is pulling to go through a hole at the line, or whether he is going to lead a play around the flank. In either case, he always runs bent over in a good blocking position, with feet wide apart to have good balance, and is constantly pulling himself along with his arms.

We try to have our pulling linemen follow given principles just as we do our linemen blocking at the line of scrimmage. When we have an offensive lineman pull and lead through a given hole in the line, we will have him turn to the inside or the outside and block the first defensive man crossing his path.

Our first and cardinal rule for downfield blocking is that an offensive blocker should never pass up one defensive man to get to another. We like to have our men blocking downfield go into every block with the intention of making contact first with a shoulder and then always keep his head between the defensive man and the path of the ball carrier. We allow them to deviate from this if they already have a good blocking angle on a defensive man, or if they come up from his blind side, which oftentimes makes a cross body block more appropriate.

I will diagram a play here in order to show how we put these principles to use in a given play. This is one of our best off-tackle plays, and we run it from both our single wing and the "T" single wing. Figure 26 shows it from the single wing formation.

When we are blocking on quick-hitting "T" plays, such as our dives, we give our linemen the very simple

principle that they are always to step for *contact* first—
never to use a position step. The only time in our
offense that we would expect a key blocker to handle
a man alone on which he didn't have an angle would
be a fast-hitting play of this type. If the defensive
man is playing head-on, the blocker will step first with
the foot in the direction he is trying to take the man,
get good contact with that shoulder, and try to bring

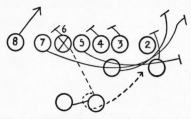

Fig. 26. Off-Tackle Blocking Principles. 2
and *wingback*—double team tackle; 3—check
block; 4—check block; *QB*—inside-out block;
5—pull through hole, block first man to inside;
6—check block; 7—pull through hole, block
first man to outside; 8—downfield block.

the opposite leg up and around to get his position on
the second step.

Drills. Now that I have covered some of the
blocking techniques, I would like to show you a few
of the drills used by some of our linemen in group
work. These basic drills are repeated daily, both in
the spring and in the fall. We like to have our offensive linemen work in units of four—the 3, 4, 5, and 7
men will work together, for example.

47

The drill for developing our lead blockers uses four dummies placed in a row a couple of yards apart, and the four offensive linemen, if making a lead block to the right, will assume a position one yard to the left of one of the dummies. On the starting count given by the line coach, they will execute the lead block all together (the four men will be hitting and executing the block at the same time). These men then hold the dummies for the next four offensive men in line, and so on. On a command of "lead block left" by the

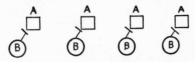

Fig. 27. Lead Blocking Drill. *A*—dummies that are being held; *B*—linemen who block dummies on starting count.

line coach, they move a yard to the right of the dummies and execute the same block with their left shoulder.

A similar drill is used for the linemen to gain proficiency in executing the inside-out block. The four linemen take a position three to four yards from their respective dummies and on a given starting count pull to the right and execute an inside-out block. After several minutes they will turn around and execute an inside-out block to the left, hitting with the opposite shoulder.

After a short time the players learn the terminology of these drills, so that as soon as they hear the words "lead block right" or "inside-out block," they know the position to assume and where to place the dummies—and there is no time lost in the preparation of the drill.

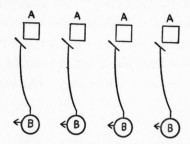

Fig. 28. Inside-Out Blocking Drill. *A*—dummies; *B*—linemen executing inside-out block on starting count.

The old two-on-one drill is one that we use a lot to give our lead blockers some contact work and post blockers an opportunity to work with the lead block-

Fig. 29. Two-on-One Drill. *A*—offensive men; *B*—defensive man; *C*—coach, who points to offensive man to be lead blocker and gives starting count.

ⒶⒶ
Ⓑ

C

ers under conditions similar to those they will meet in a game. In this drill, let the defensive man place himself wherever he wants to. A coach stands behind the defensive man and points to the offensive man who is to be the lead blocker. The other offensive man automatically becomes the post.

To make it tougher on the offensive men, we let the defensive man know the starting count. We figure if the offensive blockers can handle a defensive man who knows the starting count, they shouldn't have any trouble handling a defensive man who *doesn't* know the starting count and is waiting for the ball to react.

We give our linemen a lot of contact work, especially during pre-season training. During the season

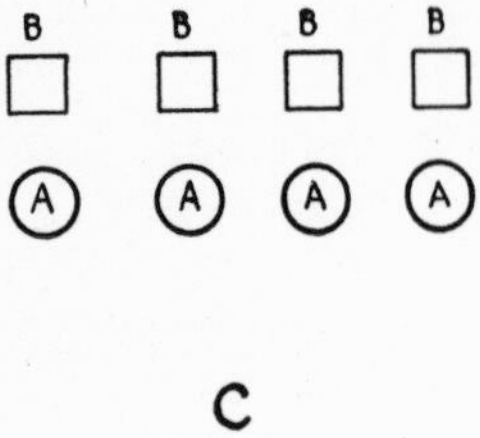

Fig. 30. Pass Protection Drill. A —offensive blockers; *B*—defensive linemen; *C*—passer.

they will get enough contact work in group practice to retain their sharpness.

The best method we have found of practicing pass protection is to pair off the offensive linemen against defensive men and have them form a pocket, staying with the defensive men and keeping the passer protected as long as possible. We make sort of a game out of this by timing them and announcing how many seconds they can keep any defensive man from touching the passer.

In working on our check blocks on the line, we have found that there is no substitute for a live one-on-one drill. The line coach stands behind the defensive men and points out the path of the ball carrier to the offensive men, and on a given signal he has them check the defensive men and try to prevent the defensive men from sliding to the ball carrier. We will have one backfield man or a lineman carrying the ball so that the defensive men will know where to react, thus making the check blocker's job as difficult as possible.

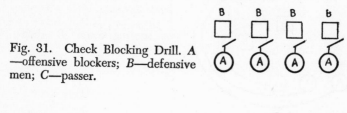

Fig. 31. Check Blocking Drill. *A* —offensive blockers; *B*—defensive men; *C*—passer.

A drill that we use almost daily in group work is one that combines pulling and downfield blocking on the starting count. Three linemen pull together in the same direction and run around a dummy that has been placed several yards to their right or left. Immediately after rounding this dummy they will turn to the inside, with the first man blocking a dummy that has been placed five yards downfield, the second man blocking another dummy that has been placed ten yards downfield, and the third man blocking a dummy

that has been placed fifteen yards downfield. These
dummies are held so that they can be blocked at top
speed by the pulling linemen. We have found that
this drill has helped to make our team take-off tremendously fast, especially on flank plays, and has done
a lot to make our boys proficient at downfield blocking.

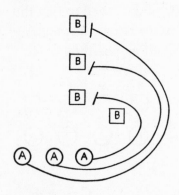

Fig. 32. Pulling and Downfield Blocking Drill. A—offensive men pulling together
on starting count; B—dum-
mies.

As you can see, we use only a few drills in the development of offensive linemen and for the practice of
our blocking techniques. The same drills are repeated over and over again with the hope that our
linemen will be able to execute their blocks and
maneuvers flawlessly.

We do not use charging sleds of any kind, although
other teams do use them to good advantage. We
like to use dummies that are facsimilies of men, so
that the blocking form used on the dummies will become automatic and apply to actual game conditions.

If I were to single out the most important phase of offensive line play, it would be the *development of team take-off*. To me, any offensive unit is only as fast as its slowest-reacting lineman.

The offensive center

Drills. Our offensive centers undergo the same rigorous drills on blocking fundamentals as the offensive guards and tackles, with the exception that we cut down the amount of time the centers spend on pulling and inside-out blocking drills. We have given our centers just a few primary blocks in our offense. We feel that his most important job is to pass the ball to the right spot at the right time and at the right speed.

It is imperative that, in our zero to 10 series, the ball be passed to the fullback's right knee. In the 20 to 30 series, the ball must be passed to the fullback's left knee. In the 30 to 40 series, the tailback must have a lead pass in the direction he is going, and, in the 40 to 50 series, the ball is soft-passed directly to the fullback's middle. In all of these instances a very small margin of error is allowed.

Because of the importance of this phase of the center's training, we have him spend a lot of time in group work with the backs, practicing the various passes that he has to make to them. Most of the blocks executed by our center are delayed or of a secondary nature. We want him to concentrate entirely on making an accurate pass and not have to be hurried in making a key block. We insist that the center have both hands on the ball at all times, whether he is passing to the quarterback in the "T," passing through the quarterback's legs to the fullback, or making a pass to any back from our single wing formation.

In teaching the center the proper grip to use, we have him take the ball, grip it as though he were going to throw a forward pass, set the ball on the ground, and then put his left hand in a position whereby he can best guide the ball accurately. We have found that it is very simple for any boy to learn to spiral a pass correctly to the fullback or tailback with this type of grip.

Stance. The stance we like to have our centers use varies with the size of the individual. We have found it advantageous to have a big man at center because it tends to widen the offensive formation and give the defense more territory to cover. When we are in our right formation we like to have the center place his right leg forward so that he can throw lead passes to his right more readily.

Position. When we are sending four receivers out on a pass play, or at any time when we are losing the fullback as a blocker on passes, due to some maneuver in the backfield, we pull our center to the short side to block the defensive end. We have him pull and head off the tail of the short-side tackle and block from the inside out on the defensive end, taking the inside angle away from the defensive man and forcing him to the outside and away from the passer.

4

Offensive End Play

The three main phases of offensive end play are *blocking, pass receiving,* and *coverage of kicks.* In our group-work drills, we allot almost equal time to blocking and pass receiving, although it is supplemented by occasional drills on kick coverage. Sometimes the ends join the linemen for group work to review play assignments and to practice those options on which they work with linemen. Often the ends join the backs for group work in connection with the passing game.

Blocking

Blocking is the basis of good football. It is of primary importance to the running game and is absolutely necessary in affording the protection required for good passing and kicking. Even tackling can be considered to be good blocking, plus the use of the hands. According to our principles we try to provide good blocking angles whenever possible, and, like other teams, we use line splits to secure these angles. Good execution is of no avail against impossible assignments.

The stance of our ends is not governed by rigid rules. We strive first for comfort and balance. A wide base is desirable, and most boys feel more comfortable with the toe of the rear foot lined up even with the heel or instep of the lead foot. The head and tail should be on the same plane. The head should be up and the eyes should be focused downfield to prevent any giveaway on assignments. The hand opposite the lead foot should be down and there should not be much weight pressed forward on that hand. The forearm on the side of the lead foot should rest on the thigh.

The most common mistake in stance is to have too

narrow a base, which destroys the balance needed. Most boys have a favorite take-off foot and will instinctively make that the lead foot in the stance. We allow our ends to assume the same stance for all plays.

At Michigan State the straight shoulder block is used almost to the exclusion of other types of blocks. We practice knee blocks and reverse blocks occasionally, but their use is supplementary to the shoulder block. In other words, *if the end misses a straight shoulder block, he tries to go immediately into a knee block or a reverse body block in a continued effort to tie up the opponent.*

Most coaches agree on the factors that constitute a good straight shoulder block. Since the team on offense has the advantage of knowing when the ball is to be snapped, they can make use of that advantage only by hitting quick and hard. Consequently, we seldom use an open-and-shut or any other type of delayed block. We think the blocker should step off with the foot nearest his opponent. The forearm nearest the opponent should be brought up hard to make a wide shoulder.

In blocking, the low man wins, so we want the end to make his contact under the shoulders of his opponent and to follow this with a lifting move, driving up through the chest of the opponent. The contact should be broad, with the ear of the blocker close against the side of his opponent. Lunging should be avoided. The feet should be up under the blocker in a wide enough spread that the blocker can make those quick foot adjustments that are necessary.

The pressure the blocker exerts should be relentless. Short digging steps should be used to drive the opponent back. Some of our ends are rather tall, and it is difficult for them to get a very low position in blocking, so in that case we encourage them to hit hard at shoulder height in an attempt to bowl the opponent over.

When a blocker double-teams with another lineman or with the wingback, another important factor enters into the execution of the block. It is absolutely necessary to "close the seam." The two blockers must keep their shoulders and hips together to prevent the defensive man from splitting them and causing them to block against each other. When the end and wingback are blocking a tackle, we make the end responsible for the first contact and want him to prevent any penetration by the defensive man.

Since variations occur in the position of the defensive tackle, we do not specify which foot the wingback shall use to step off. It is much more important that he try to get under the shoulder of the tackle and press in against the end to keep that seam closed. We try to take the tackle back, and, if the two blockers can get a really favorable position, they try to drive the tackle in at the same time. We don't use any kind of "high-low" blocks.

On a flank play it is sometimes necessary for an end to cut off a man who has a position outside of him, and in this situation we use what we call an *outside block*. For instance, if the right end must block an opponent who is to his outside, he should drive in to the defensive man in an effort to make contact as quickly as possible. The blocker's head should go past the opponent on his outside and the contact should be with the inside, or left, shoulder. This should be followed by a quick adjustment of the feet in an attempt to end up in a regular straight shoulder block with an outside position on the opponent. If the opponent plays so far outside of the end that the assignment is impossible, the end should make contact from the inside and drive the opponent out, relying upon the ball carrier to take advantage of the block.

There is a temptation on this block to use an open-and-shut technique, but against a good defensive lineman this is not effective. The opponent often catches the end in an unbalanced position and drives through or past him. If the end meets a "submarine" type of defensive charge, he merely smothers the defensive man with his knees and body.

In applying the knee block, the end should drive his upper thigh well up into the crotch of his opponent, and the blocker's hands and feet should make contact with the ground as he "crabs" the block. In applying the reverse block, the ends should make shoulder contact first, then go into the reverse, keeping his hip high against the side of the opponent. This block too should be "crabbed" to maintain the pressure on the defensive man.

To block linebackers, the ends should employ the same two types of blocks used by the linemen. The driving block, or the one by which we move a defensive man, should be applied with good position and balance. It is often necessary to anticipate the movement of the linebacker, and sometimes the offense must use a reverse block rather than a straight shoulder block.

As a general rule, we want the block on the linebackers to be applied rather high, and we stress the importance of keeping the pressure on the defensive man. We tell them that *one more fraction of a second may mean a long run.*

The position block on the linebacker is like a pass protection block. After the end gets position, he should make whatever adjustments are necessary to stay between the defensive man and the ball carrier, and cut off recovery by the defensive man.

In downfield blocking *timing* is the most important single factor. *It is useless to knock down a defensive man too soon.* Many of the most effective downfield blocks are running blocks in which the blocker keeps on his feet and allows the ball carrier to use him as a screen or a post. When there is an opportunity to surprise a man in the secondary, a long body block is probably the most effective. Downfield blocking is discouraging work when so many plays end at the line of scrimmage. These boys must be constantly reminded that *their* block may be the one that brings in the winning touchdown.

Sometimes an end is called upon in pass or punt protection to put on the same type of block that a lineman uses in similar circumstances. The policy on this type of block is to hit, give a step, hit again, and so on. The blocker should keep the opponent to his outside and should attempt to drive him back past the passer. As a last resort in protecting a passer, an all-out effort should be made to make any contact possible with arms, legs, or any other part of the body, right up to the last second. Here again, one more second may allow the passer to throw a touchdown pass.

A very good rule in football is to *keep on your feet.* This applies equally to offensive and defensive players, and it is very important to good blocking. Boys who lunge or leave their feet for any other reason are out of the game, but anyone who stays on his feet can still be helpful to his team. Blocking is the hard work of football, but those who do it well should take great pride in their ability.

Blocking drills are a daily part of our group work for ends. We usually start with a five-minute session on the big bags. This serves as a warmup for the shoulders and it gives the coach a chance to observe form and "pop." All types of blocks are reviewed. Then we pair the players off, and on a coach's signal half of the group blocks the others in man-to-man "live" blocking. The coach calls out a play number and the blockers execute the particular type of block needed on that play.

We encourage the defensive men to be rough, and we emphasize getting under the shoulder of the opponent and hitting and lifting on the block. This is followed by a session against linebackers. We give the linebackers a pad that they hold about waist-high and encourage them to move around so the ends must make quick foot adjustments in order to get contact with them.

We stress staying with the block and tell the ends that sometimes another fraction of a second of pressure may be responsible for a long run. Dummy scrimmage gives the end coach an opportunity to check assignments very carefully and to insist upon correct blocking form.

Pass receiving

Our ends spend part of every practice session on some phase of the passing game. Sometimes they merely run the patterns of opponents when our major attention is on pass defense. At other times the emphasis is entirely upon our own passing offense. Most boys like to catch passes, and in the warmup period before practice begins the ends get in a lot of pass receiving.

To be good receivers the ends must be relaxed and loose. We want them to catch the ball with their hands. As a general rule we suggest that passes above the waist be caught with thumbs in, below the waist with thumbs out. To receive a ball over the shoulder, with the receiver running in the same direction as the ball is thrown, it is probably easier to catch it with the thumbs out.

It is surprising to see the number of boys who have not learned to get off the ground in an attempt to catch a high pass. Sometimes a boy who is otherwise a fine receiver has not learned to make the necessary foot adjustments that allow him to leap off the ground for a high one, so we take a few minutes now and then to throw a few high ones and encourage them to go all-out to make the catch.

We want the end to try hard to catch every ball, no matter how far out of his reach it may appear. There is no substitute for confidence, and to protect this quality we minimize his misses. We try to give the receivers the impression that catching the ball is a very minor accomplishment, and that any boy can do it.

There is a growing tendency by the defense to hold up receivers at the line of scrimmage. To overcome this, we use several maneuvers. In the first place, even at the risk of giving away our intent, we want the receivers to split out, if necessary, to get out into those pass lanes or patterns, for this gives us a chance to complete the pass even though the defense has been warned. If an end allows himself to be held up, it becomes almost impossible to complete a pass no matter how good the deception is.

Another maneuver that we encourage is the quick head-and-shoulder fake opposite the direction the receiver wants to take. Or, the end may make contact with the opponent and pivot quickly away toward the direction we want him to take.

Another method of breaking free is to scramble on the hands and feet for a couple of yards and then get up and go. If it is not necessary to get very far downfield, we can sometimes put on a full block and then go to the pass lane. We also have a couple of running plays that we use to take advantage of a holdup. In one game in 1951, one of our reverse plays was responsible for gains totaling almost 200 yards because a defensive linebacker was so intent upon holding up our end from the inside.

We spend a lot of time practicing evasive maneuvers in connection with our pass patterns. Some boys can make very good use of the change of pace, and we encourage all of them to learn to use it. Other boys are more effective with a head-and-shoulder fake or with the old "Z" pattern. Another evasive movement we practice is the "hook-and-go." The ends should get fairly close to the defender before using an evasive maneuver, because that is where it is most effective. If a defender backs away quickly, it is comparatively easy to use the hook, or stop, pattern on him.

In practicing hook passes we caution the end to be sure to get a reasonable depth. If the down is third and eight, we don't want him to hook at six yards. Most hook receivers are tackled in their tracks, so we caution them to turn immediately after the catch and head for the goal line. Boys who try to swing back toward the line of scrimmage to avoid tacklers often lose all of the ground they originally gained. The hook man should face the passer with his knees slightly bent, and should be relaxed so that he can jump for a high one or go to the side for an inaccurate pass.

We want our receivers to run sharp breaking patterns rather than curves. The decoys should run hard, be good actors, and be ready to catch the ball if it is thrown to them. When the pass has been thrown to another receiver, the decoy should turn immediately to try to do some helpful blocking. Pass receivers should stay far enough away from each other that they can not be covered by one defensive man.

Finally, we encourage them to score after they have

caught the ball. They should use a straight-arm, pivot, and dodge, and make every effort to go all of the way with the pass. Too many boys seem to be satisfied merely to make the catch.

In our offensive pass drills we spend a few moments practicing the maneuvers to get away from a holdup, then we run a man-on-man drill that gives our receiver a chance to practice evasive maneuvers. When backs are not available for group work with ends we have the ends take turns as defensive backs. This helps us to convince our receivers how difficult it is for a defensive back to stay with a clever receiver. Later these maneuvers are attempted against our defensive backs, and execution must be better if the end is to get free.

In group work with the backs, the ends engage in skeleton drills, which afford an opportunity to practice complete patterns. Exact lanes are stressed in this drill, and a difference of a yard or so becomes very important as the pattern develops. For a little fun, we have a drill, called "50-straight" that we play whenever time permits. Passers and receivers both try hard to complete 50 straight passes, and the boy who drops one when the count gets up into the 30's really catches it from his teammates.

Covering kicks

Covering kicks is a very important phase of the game of football. The safety man for the opponent is generally the very best runner they have, and poor coverage may cost the team a surprising yardage total. The ends must first recognize their responsibility for protection if the closed punt formation is used. When the kicker is right-footed, the left end must protect before he goes downfield to cover the punt. He blocks the first defensive man who lines up outside the protecting back on his side. The closer this defensive man is to the kicker, the more definite the block by the end must be. The right end, in this case, should take any split that will permit him to get downfield quickly.

Ends who are covering kicks should go hard, be rough with the hands on the defensive backs, keep blockers away from the legs and ankles, and above all, should keep on their feet. They should attempt to get to the point that gives them an angle on the receiver, and from that point they should work to force the receiver to run toward the other end. One of the most common mistakes is overrunning the receiver. Another bad one is to be caught inside and allow the runner to get out to the sidelines. *The end's primary responsibility is to turn the receiver toward the other tacklers.*

Against a criss-cross return, the end should make himself responsible for the back who comes his way. He should be careful about looking up to see the direction of the kick. Many backs are taught to wait for this and then to move in on the end as he gazes skyward.

The end should be thoroughly familiar with the rules that apply to this particular phase of the game. He can look pretty foolish if he tackles the receiver before the ball arrives, or if he gets hit on the head by the punt, or if he downs a rolling punt inside the opponent's ten-yard line!

5

Backfield Play

The Michigan State multiple offense is stimulating and enjoyable for our backs to play. It offers a wide variety of techniques and skills to master. On the surface these techniques and skills may look difficult and impossible to teach, but we have found it just the opposite. We feel that by use of drills, proper introduction of sequence, repetition of plays, and good attention on the part of the boys, that the teaching of all the techniques we use can be successful.

Stance

The backfield stance used by Michigan State varies to a degree with the formation used. In our single wing (100 formation) with the wingback stationed just outside the end, we use the two-point stance for our left halfback, fullback, and quarterback. We ask that their feet and knees be as wide as their shoulders, and that the weight be evenly distributed on the balls of their feet. We also require the eyes to be pointed straight downfield. The palms of the hands rest lightly on the knees, which are bent.

Certain boys will vary a little from this stance. By checking for results, leeway is granted whereby the feet are sometimes a little wider in this position than that we normally ask a boy to take. When we use the deep wing formation the right halfback assumes the same stance as the other three backs.

The first formation we will discuss is the "100." The wingback should be stationed 12 inches outside his offensive end and 12 inches back. This placement should remain constant regardless of the end shift, especially the 12-inch space back from the end. We find that if he moves up at all, he makes the end ineligible for forward passes. We allow this halfback to get down to a three-point position with his left leg back and his left arm down. We find that this gives us an advantage when it comes to blocking the tackle with the end wing block. For spacing of backs see Illustration 1, page 83.

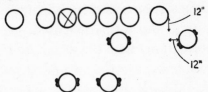

Fig. 33. The "100" Formation.

The second single wing formation that we use at Michigan State is the backwing, or as we refer to it, the *zero formation.* The stance of the left halfback, fullback, and quarterback is the same as that of our 100

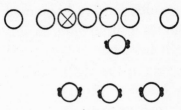

Fig. 34. The "Zero" Formation.

formation. We now space the right halfback on a straight line with the left halfback and fullback and have him in a two-point stance. On reverses his timing in this formation will vary from the 100 formation, however. This timing is worked on very carefully to make it synchronize with the full spin of the fullback.

. Our quarterback in the "T" takes a square stance directly behind the center, much after the fashion of the "split-T" quarterbacks. His feet and knees are approximately 18 inches apart, and this space allows the ball to be centered between his legs; he also is in a position to handle the ball from the center on a direct exchange. We ask the quarterback to have his thumbs together and his fingers open, with the backs of his hands along the inside seam of the trousers of the center. The quarterback should stand tall and,

Fig. 35.   The Conventional "T" Formation.

as he takes his preliminary position, should always look from left to right and try and detect any defensive spacings of which he may later take advantage.

The halfbacks and fullbacks are in a straight line approximately 4½ yards from the ball, forming the conventional "T." They assume the two-point stance with their head and eyes pointing straight forward. The halfbacks do not watch the ball; however, the fullback does. The reason for this is that the ball sometimes is centered directly to the fullback, and we want him always to be giving his 100 per cent attention to this possibility.

In teaching the stance for both the "T" and the single wing, we go into a great deal of detail in lining the boys up in two straight lines and then having our backfield coach walk around them and correct their positions. Coaching points that are again noted are the position of the feet, bend of the knees, position of the hands, and so on.

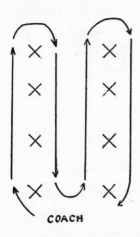

Fig. 36. The backfield coach walks around the backs and corrects their stance.

A variation of our "T" formation occurs when we take the right halfback from his conventional "T" and place him in a wingback position that is 12 inches back and 12 inches in from the end, much after the fashion of our wingback in the 100 formation. We now ask the wingback to get down into his three-point stance inside of the back. The quarterback, fullback, and left halfback are in a two-point stance, the same as in our "T" formation.

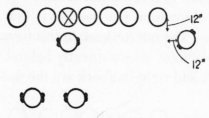

Fig. 37. The "T" 100 Formation.

Here it should be pointed out again that timing plays a great part in our offense. The reverse plays, in particular, are a little out of time now and then, and caution should be taken to correct the spin of the fullback to compensate for this timing difference.

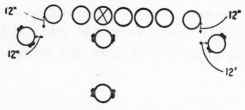

Fig. 38. The Double Wing Formation.

In our double wing formation, we ask the left halfback and right halfback to take a three-point stance just 12 inches outside of their ends. In both cases the inside leg is back and the inside arm is down. A quarterback takes his conventional square stance of the "T" formation with his hands underneath the crotch of the center. The fullback is lined up directly behind the quarterback in a two-point stance.

The fifth formation that we use is that of the left halfback up. The quarterback in this formation takes a square, two-point stance directly behind the center. The fullback and right halfback are the same as in our

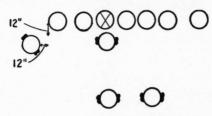

Fig. 39. The Left Half Up Formation.

conventional "T" formation. Our left halfback now assumes the same position as he did on our double wing, that is, 12 inches outside his end and 12 inches back. His inside arm is down and his inside leg is back.

Shift

In order to get from one formation to another, we use a three-count shift, i.e., "1-2-3." In teaching the three-count shift, we teach by the following method: On the count of "1," we ask the boys who are to shift to lift the lead leg and place it in the direction in which they are going. We caution them to have the foot lifted and *down* on the count of 1. On the count of "2" we use a cross-over. When the boys hear "two" we want the cross-over foot *down* and *planted*. On the count of "3" we ask that *both* feet be down on the ground. There must be absolutely no movement.

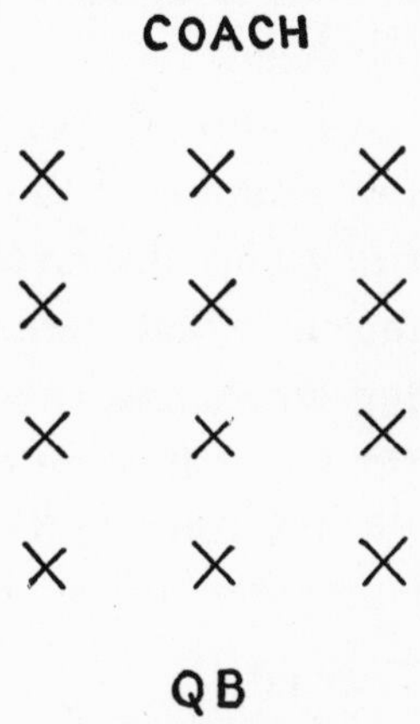

COACH

X   X   X

Fig. 40. The position of the quar-   X   X   X
terback teaching the three-count
shift.
X   X   X

X   X   X

QB

In teaching this drill we line up our entire group of backs and have the quarterback step out in front and count his cadence. We give a short shift right, or a short shift left—or, a long shift right or a long shift left. It is not done with any thought of creating a formation at that moment, however. We are merely laying the foundation for a future shift.

It should be noted that in our formation all of our backs do not shift the same distance. By proper teaching we find that we can ask certain boys to adjust to the shift required of them because of their background of learning the long and short shift. Although we are primarily a right-formation team, we have run a great deal from the left-formation in the past, hence the long and short shift to the left.

In watching the entire group count, we pay a great deal of attention to excessive bobbing or dropping of the head, or any poor movement on the part of the boys. Proper corrections are made on the spot. A few minutes of this work each day will enable the entire group of men to make any sort of shift without the mistakes that were just as described. When this shifting movement can be accomplished smoothly, formations that involve shifting are practiced—for example, the 100 formation or deep wing formation.

Take-off

To us, the proper take-off is one of the major points in good backfield play. We spend an exceptional amount of time in teaching the take-off, whether it be from the "T," the single wing, or any of our other formations. To teach our lateral movements we use a drill whereby we line the boys up in a straight line with their right foot touching the line of scrimmage (see Figure 41).

We ask the boys to turn and push, and, at the same time, gain six inches in the direction that they are going. The reason for the white line is that, as a boy turns and pushes, he will invariably lose ground with his lead step. Corrections can be made on the spot. The opposite procedure is used when we want a boy to learn to go to his left. Our saying is "Turn and push" on "Ready hike 1-2-3." This drill can be done in the same way to the right and left.

By constant work and repetition we try to achieve the take-off that we want. We ask the backs to do this drill at top speed. At this point, I would like to em-

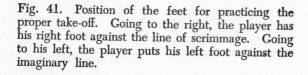

Fig. 41. Position of the feet for practicing the proper take-off. Going to the right, the player has his right foot against the line of scrimmage. Going to his left, the player puts his left foot against the imaginary line.

phasize a coaching point that we make to our backs at least four times each day. That is, *we want them to do everything at top speed,* feeling that we can slow down on Saturdays but that we cannot speed up. We find that if boys will practice their drills with this in mind, we do get additional smoothness and much better performance on the day of the game.

Our "T" take-off is primarily a forward movement of the halfbacks and we like to have them move as quickly as possible. Emphasis is placed on the backs' moving their feet before they move the body. Bringing their feet up very high or shuffling their feet is discouraged. We have experimented, at times with having both halfbacks place the inside leg back slightly and have asked them to take their push-off from their front leg.

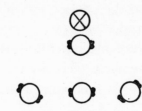

Fig. 42. The position of the feet for backs in the "T" formation.

When these techniques can be mastered, it is a sign of arriving at the point of achievement in the take-off that we want. Again, only by having the backs repeat these quick movements constantly do we feel that we have increased their take-off time.

Exchanges

Single wing exchange. During our single wing exchange we ask the man who receives the ball to form a pocket over or just below the belt of his trousers. His little fingers should have a space of two inches between them, and his thumbs should be pointed in the same direction as his shoulders. The backs of his hands should be two inches from his body. We call this the *receiving position* for the single wing.

We emphasize that, when receiving, the receiver not look at the ball because the responsibility for giving the ball correctly is placed on the giver. The giver places the ball into the pocket with his hand directly in the center of and on the back panel of the ball.

In the drill used to teach this exchange, we place the boys in two lines approximately fifteen yards apart, facing each other. An exchange point is agreed upon

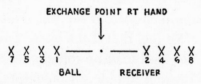

Fig. 43. Exchange drill for single wing exchange.

roughly. Then we have the boys move at half-speed and make the exchange. Player No. 1 gives to player No. 2, player No. 2 gives to player No. 3, and so on. It is recommended that this drill be done at half-speed or less so that it can be used for coaching purposes. For example, when two boys are coming toward each other and one boy is 6'1" and the other 5'7", the adjustment of levels must be taken into consideration. This same situation could occur in a football game in which a fullback might be 6'1" and the left halfback 5'7".

As soon as the right hand-off has been used a given number of times, the left-hand exchange must be added. This drill is used by our backs every day of spring practice and every day of fall practice.

"T" Exchange. Our "T" exchange varies a great deal from our single wing exchange. We ask that the inside arm of the boy going past the quarterback be up underneath the receiver's chin. We take the opposite arm, bend it at the elbow, and lay it across the body (see Illustrations 21 and 22, page 89).

Both palms are facing each other. The lower arm should be three inches from the body with the palm straight up. We feel that if the lower arm is in tight to the body, the ball may be rolled over the forearm and thereby cause a fumble. Conversely, if it is out nine inches, the giver may put the ball straight through, again causing a fumble.

We work a great deal on the quarterback placing the ball into the stomach and then pulling it out. In drills we seldom tell the halfback receiving the ball that he will receive it. We leave it up to the quarterback to determine whether he will give the ball or merely place it in there and pull it out.

Great care should be taken that men receiving the ball pass on both sides of the quarterback. Another coaching point is that *the quarterback is responsible for placing the ball in our "T" exchange*, thereby allowing the receiver to better utilize his eyes.

Illus. 1.   Single Wing Formation, Wingback Deep.   (*See p. 9.*)

Illus. 2.   Single Wing Formation, Wingback Up.   (*See p. 8.*)

Illus. 3.   The "T" Formation.   (*See pp. 12 and 73.*)

Illus. 4.   The "T" 100 Formation.   (*See pp. 26-27 and 75.*)

Illus. 5.   The "T" Double Wing.   (*See pp. 28-29.*)

Illus. 6.   The "124 Play," Defensive View.   (*See pp. 112-114.*)

Illus. 7. The "122 Play," Defensive View.

Illus. 8. The "122 Play," Offensive View.

Illus. 9. The "124 Play," Offensive View.

Illus. 10. The Huddle.
(*See p. 33.*)

Illus. 11. Lead Post
Block. No. 55 is the
lead blocker. (*See p.
39.*)

Illus. 12. The Offensive Stance.

Illus. 13.   The First Step of a Lead Block Right.

Illus. 14.   The Second Step of a Lead Block Right.

Illus. 15.   Check Blocking with Use of the Crab Block.

Illus. 16 (*left, above*). An end receives an on-and-over pass. He keeps his thumbs out, his hands relaxed, and his eyes on the ball. Illus. 17 (*right, above*). An end-wingback block on a tackle. Shoulders and hips are together, and the end is exerting a full block. The wingback is beginning the lateral drive. Notice the closed seam.

Illus. 18 (*left, above*). An outside block. The blocker has taken his second step, has driven his head past the outside hip of his opponent, and is ready to take up a full outside angle. Notice the straight shoulder contact. Illus. 19 (*right, above*). Continuing with an outside block, the blocker has taken one more quick step with his right foot and now has full blocking position for the flank play.

Illus. 20. Two-point
Backfield Stance.

Illus. 21. The "T" Ex-
change.

Illus. 22. Pocket for
Single Wing Exchange.

Illus. 23. The Halfback Receiving the Ball on a "T" Exchange.

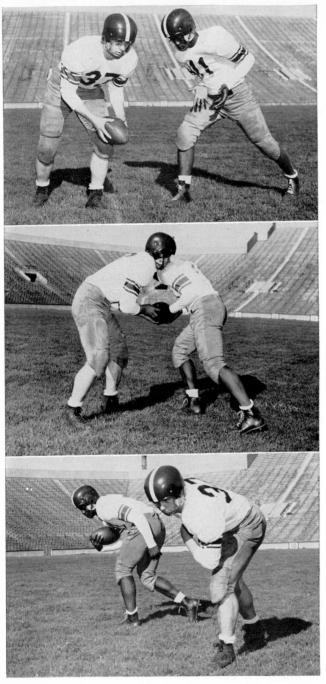

Illus. 24. These three pictures show the three steps for a full spin and give to the left half by the fullback. (*See Chapter 5.*)

Illus. 25.   The " 'T' 100, Left End Cross."
The picture shows the pass protection with
the center as free man and the passer in
the pocket.   Decoys are clearing the area
for the No. 1 receiver, the left end.

Illus. 26.   A Tie-up Block for a Halfback.

Illus. 27.   The Rollout Pass, Right End Out.
The protection is working away from the
passer's area.   The left half, No. 62, continues in a flare pattern to be the fourth receiver.   The passer keys off the defensive
halfback.

Illus. 28.   Evan Slonac hurdling a group of Penn State players in a 1952 game.

Illus. 29.   Billy Wells, 1952, makes 19 yards versus the University of Michigan with a reverse play.

Illus. 30.   Pisano, 1951, runs a reverse play against Oregon State.   No. 58 is Frank Kapral.

Illus. 31.   Sonny Grandelius, All-American, 1951, is shown about to lateral as he is being tackled in the Minnesota-Michigan State game.

Illus. 32. Lynn Chadnois, All American in 1949, getting away from a Michigan tackler.

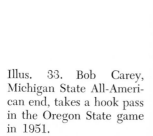

Illus. 33. Bob Carey, Michigan State All-American end, takes a hook pass in the Oregon State game in 1951.

Our exchange for the zero formation is exactly the same as our exchange for our 100 formation. We refer to this as our single wing exchange. We check very closely to make sure that the boys conform to the correct method of exchange. Any time they are confused, it is brought to their attention immediately by the use of drills. We feel that they are always able to perfect the single wing exchange.

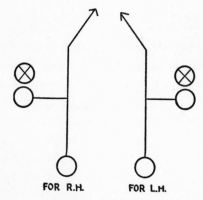

FOR R.H. FOR L.H.

Fig. 44. Drill for the "T" Exchange.
The quarterback stands to the side.

Our "T" 100 exchange with the quarterback handling the ball conforms to our conventional "T" exchange. We again place the responsibility on the quarterback as the giver, and we charge the receiver with forming the pocket.

During our double wing exchange, in which the

quarterback is underneath the center, we tie in the exchange with our "T" and our "T" 100. This also holds true for our left halfback formation.

To summarize the exchange, we say that we use the single wing exchange any time we are in the zero or 100 formation; and that we will use the "T" exchange on the "T" formation, "T" 100, double wing, and left halfback up formations.

Spinning

The three-count spin is used at Michigan State. Particularly, we use a three-point spin for our fullback. On our spin to the left we ask the fullback to point his left foot toward the sideline, and while opening this

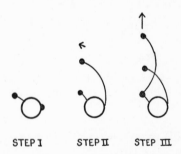

STEP I STEP II STEP III

Fig. 45. The correct foot-work for the three-count spin.

foot he gains three inches with it. This is done on the count of "One." Secondly, we ask him to swing his right leg around so that his right toe comes underneath his right shoulder and is pointed at a 90-degree angle from where he started. On the third step, we ask him to pivot on the balls of his feet and swing the left leg, placing the toe in the direction that he is going. The correct footwork of the second and third steps is most important.

Great care should be taken to use proper spacing. We have found that if, on his second step, a boy puts his right leg too far forward, that his third step will be

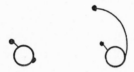

Fig. 46. Incorrect foot-work on the second step of the three-count spin.

entirely out of proportion, thereby causing a poor spin.

In teaching this drill, we line the fullbacks up on a chalk line. The backfield coach walks behind the group and counts "1-2-3." He has the boys simulate the full spin as they progress up and down the field.

We also use a spin to the right in which we reverse the procedure. Care should be taken again, however, that both drills not be given during the same week. A boy's progress is noted, and when he has mastered the art of turning around to his left, the second drill may be brought in. The boys go up and down the chalk

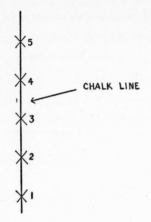

Fig. 47. Three-count Spin Drill.

COACH – COUNTS + CORRECTS

line keeping good body balance. Later in the week, hands are introduced into the footwork drill. This will be explained later in this chapter when we take up the "124 play."

Blocking

Our backs are called upon to do their share of blocking in our offense. Our blocking is taught mainly with large bags. In giving instruction we try to have each boy simulate the type of block he will use in the ball game.

We start with the halfbacks blocking ends as they might do on an end sweep or a long reverse. We call this a tie-up block (see Illustration 26, page 91).

98

When teaching this blocking, we have the half-backs approach directly the man that he is to block, without letting this defensive man know whether he is going to be blocked in or out. At the last moment we slide the shoulder on beyond the hip of the end and hook with the thigh and hip. We ask our players to fall into a high "crab" block and keep working. Great care is taken that the elbow does not get into a position whereby offensive holding may be called.

While the halfbacks are working on their tie-up block, we will have the quarterbacks working on inside-out blocks, which, to us, are shoulder blocks. Actually, the blocking of our quarterbacks is primarily that of shoulder blocking.

Our fullback, in the meantime, may be working on a block which is primarily a tie-up block. He is asked to block according to the type of play that is being called. For example, if he were blocking an end on an end sweep, he would use his tie-up block, while if he were asked to block an end out on an off-tackle play, he would be working on a shoulder block. Whenever he is to double-team with a linesman or another back, we always have the two men work together on double-team shoulder blocks. Blocking and ball-carrying mean exactly the same to us. We know that the ball cannot be moved without fine blocking from the entire team.

99

Additional drills

Like all people who play football, we have our trouble hanging on to the ball. We spend a great deal of time in asking our boys to put the ball away. We tell them very definitely that the ball should not be carried out in one hand or in *any* position where it is away from the body. To emphasize this we set up what we call our *gauntlet drill*.

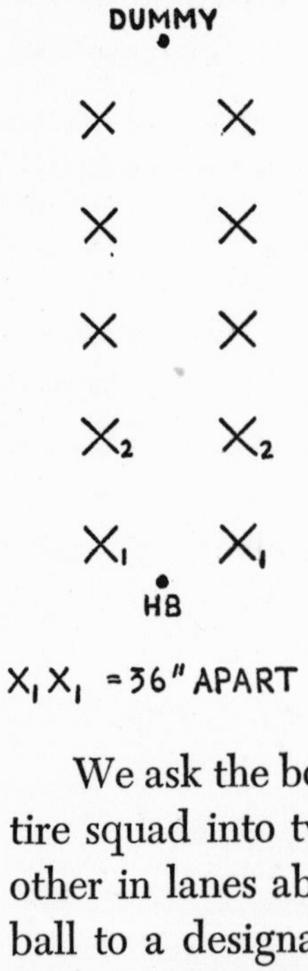

DUMMY

X   X

X   X

X   X   Fig. 48. Gauntlet drill used to teach backs to hold on to the ball.

X_2 X_2

X_1 X_1
HB

$X_1 X_1$ = 36" APART

We ask the boys to form a gauntlet dividing the entire squad into two groups with one group facing the other in lanes about a yard apart. Then we give the ball to a designated back and have him run through the gauntlet where his teammates try to tear the ball from his grasp. This emphasizes the fact that *we want the ball put away*. Many times we place a dummy at the farthest end of the gauntlet and have the boy slam into this as he emerges.

A few times during the season, we ask that men forming the gauntlet get down on one knee and grab for the ball. We feel that this simulates the game condition where a lineman who has been knocked down reaches up and tears for the ball as the ball carrier is running past his position. Great care should be taken that this drill be run very rapidly, and each boy should

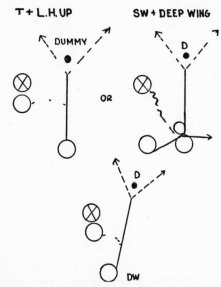

Fig. 49. The backs simulate various timing situations and explode into the dummy for further practice in hanging on to the ball.

not be asked to go through more than three times at the most. Otherwise, the boys reaching for the ball will not always give an honest effort, owing to their fingernails being broken or hand wounds received while reaching for the ball.

Another drill that has been very successful has the backs run at a man who holds the heaviest bag we have. This drill is done from each of our formations. We ask the backs to explode into this dummy and then

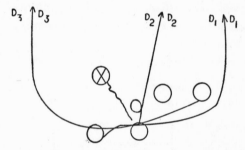

Fig. 50. Two men slam their dummies as the ball carrier passes through. The ball carrier learns to hold onto the ball under any condition.

pivot. We set this up with one man holding the bag on the line of scrimmage, thereby causing the ball carrier to make contact while not always having control of the ball. We move the bag-holder back and forward to set up various timing situations.

Another drill that we like very much uses six freshmen boys who come up and hold large bags (see Figure 50). The job of the bag holders is to insure that the ball carrier put the ball away when in trouble.

We ask the boys to work in pairs, placing the first pair of dummies about a yard off the line of scrimmage and at the approximate position of our 1-hole. The second group of boys will have the same position only they will be placed at approximately the 4-hole. The third group of two boys should be placed at the 9-hole. We ask these boys to have roughly 30 inches between the two bags that they are working on. Then on our command, the left halfback will simulate an end run and run between the bags (D_1D_1).

We ask the bag holders to slam the bags together to shock the ball carriers, thus again emphasizing that the boy must put the ball away when running into trouble. The same drill is done as the fullback goes up the center of the formation and runs between D_2D_2. We have the right halfs run what we consider a reverse or a "9 play" (D_3D_3). Naturally, these bags can be moved a little to the right or to the left so that each hole is given a good workout. The approximate position of the backs is again one yard off the line of scrimmage, and this gives a boy a full chance to get up full steam by the time he smacks into the center of the two bags on which he is working. We also set this drill up from our "T" and other formations.

The fourth drill that we work on concerns (1) picking up loose balls, and (2) the correct method of falling on them. Many times it is taken for granted that a boy knows how to fall on or how to pick up a loose ball. We try to take precautions that a boy is checked-out with the correct method of recovering his own or his opponent's fumble. If there is to be any experimenting, we would rather have it done on the practice field rather than in an important game.

Running techniques

Running in the secondary. Everything that we have done up to this time has been aimed at getting the ball carrier up to and through the line of scrimmage with good ball-handling techniques. We have a drill at Michigan State that we like very much which deals with running into the secondary. We take our defensive secondary and place them in a defensive position. We use the linebackers, deep men, and ends.

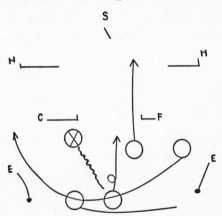

Fig. 51. Practice running in the secondary. The defenders tag the runner.

The offensive quarterback takes his skeleton backfield and calls an offensive play that will be run into the secondary. We tell the offensive backs to run for a touchdown, and at the same time we have the defensive men try to tag the ball carriers. We watch the pursuit of the defense, and during this drill we try to teach correct running for a long touchdown to the ball carrier. The offensive men get a great deal of practice in field position running, especially in regard to sideline, down, distance, and approach in secondary. It should be mentioned that a defensive coach is placed with a defensive team while an offensive coach is placed with an offensive team, because great work can be done from an offensive and defensive standpoint in this way.

Change of pace. We talk to all of our backs about a change of pace. This, of course, is an individual skill, but it is an important phase of successful offensive running. We define "change of pace" as that little bit in reserve to *step on and beyond* the man trying to make the tackle. Sometimes a head fake, a shoulder fake, or a shrug of the hips may be sufficient; however, we have found that good defensive tacklers do not take this fake because they are watching the belt buckle of the runner. A change of pace combined with a shrug of the hips will pay great dividends.

Straight-arm. The straight-arm is not stressed a great deal at Michigan State because we are great believers in lowering the shoulder and trying to get every bit of yardage we can. We do have a method of dropping the inside shoulder and hanging the arm straight down about six inches from the thigh and keeping it in that position. As a defensive man approaches and tries to wind his arms around the legs of the ball carrier, we ask the runner to take this hanging arm and use it to keep the defensive man from getting a grip on the thighs by having the defense tackle the arm. The arm can be used as a club to keep the defensive man from getting the contact that he wants. We feel that this is a fine drill for a big strong back; it is not recommended for a smaller boy who would be overpowered by a good, hard defensive tackle.

Pivots. Pivots are worked on a great deal, however. Each coach should spend a considerable amount of time having a boy pivot under simulated actual game conditions. A fine drill for this is to have a boy run down along the sidelines and have a defensive man corner him. Obviously, if he continues along the sidelines, he will be driven out of bounds. A good alternative is to use a pivot giving the leg and taking it away, then cutting back and pivoting into the secondary. We have found that in college the pursuit of the linemen discourages this to a certain degree; however, if the condition is there, it should be tried. Care should be given that this drill, or any running drill, be thoroughly tested and proven in a boy's mind before submitting it to game conditions.

Cutbacks. Cutbacks are a common part of our repertoire. Through design, we tell a boy whether he should cut back or cut out. By *design* we mean we tell the runner what we want him to do as the play is being given on the board. We tell him that his blockers are coming from this angle or that angle, and on certain plays he should get on the outside while on other plays he should get to the inside.

Suggestions for the ball carrier

We have three major suggestions for ball carriers. I know there are many more, but I would like to cover at least these three.

We feel that the only time a back should slow down is for the *timing of a play or to pick up blockers.* By *timing* we mean that we have a certain number of plays in which we try to fool the defense into thinking that we are taking three or four steps and then stopping. What we are doing, really, is lulling the defense; at the last moment these blockers speed up and the ball carriers picks them up. If a ball carrier is taking a hand-off or is running some type of play where he must get in behind these blockers, it would involve slowing down to time our play.

The second vital thing we stress very heavily is that our backs are not to point by leaning or by use of eyes. We feel that we have thoroughly indoctrinated each boy about when to take off and where to go that he does not have to take an unfair advantage by leaning or anticipating his next move. I would like to stress a slogan that we have, and that is *"Know what to do and do it hard."* Leaning and pointing with the eyes or any other part of the body indicates clearly a lack of grasp of fundamentals.

The third thing we ask our backs to do is have a strong running base. We like the type of boy who runs close to the ground. We feel that we cannot be successful with a boy who carries his weight high, because as he is tackled he goes down too easily. We favor the type of boy with a strong base who, when hit, can keep his base or at least can regain it quickly and go on for considerably more yardage.

Passing

All of our passers are classified by the staff into categories. We try to determine whether they are long passers, short passers, and so on. Our passing game is really built around these findings. We check the grip and footwork used by Michigan State and have the boys use a drill that will allow us to observe the grip and technique of the passer.

In teaching passing, we always ask all passers to throw the ball back and forth from a formation similar to the old cross-court drill in basketball, where one group is about twenty feet from another. We tell them to bring both hands up to the right ear, providing, of course, they are right-handed. We stress the position of the feet, and as they throw, we check the

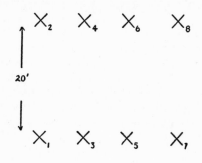

X₁ PASSES TO X₂ ETC

Fig. 52.   Passing Practice.

body balance and make corrections. Again, if they have had great success with their throwing, we try to evaluate this and make recommendations from our findings. Passing will be covered in another chapter, and we will not pursue this topic further at this time, except to say that when working on pass protection, the backfield should work with the line and ends, and pass protection should be carried on as a team exercise rather than a group project. The same recommenda-

109

tion applies to the offensive passing game, which will be discussed in a later chapter, the recommendation being that when putting in pass plays the passer work with the ends and the backs in all pass patterns.

It is strongly advised that the boys you are counting on be placed together when giving out passing assignments, and that a good portion of time be allotted to this phase of the offensive game.

Putting the backfield together

Centering the ball is of great importance when putting the backfield together in our multiple offense. At Michigan State, the duties of the line coach and backfield coach overlap in this respect. The line coach has the duty of teaching blocking assignments, while the backfield coach is responsible for the center's passing technique.

A word should be said about centering in our multiple offense. Probably the most difficult job for the center is to be able to center the ball accurately on so many different plays. For example, his skill is called upon to send the ball to the left knee of the fullback on a spin to the left, right knee of the fullback on a spin to the right, belt buckle of the fullback on the wedge plays, and so on; and he must place the ball correctly in the quarterback's hands on the "T" exchange and other plays of type.

In putting the backfield together, a major percentage of our time is devoted to a skeleton backfield drill. In this drill, we have the opportunity to check fundamentals, techniques, and proper assignments. Here backs are placed together with a center, and plays are run as designated by an assistant coach. If three backfields are available, three separate groups may be working at the same time. If two backfields are available, then two groups should be working.

The assistant coach should direct the calling of plays, and each group should run the same play. As mistakes are made the play should always be corrected and run over. If one group misses an assignment, all groups should be penalized because there is no substitute for repetition in football. A successful quotation in athletics is, "Tell them once and then have them do it a million times, rather than tell them a million times and have them do it once."

Care should be taken that *all plays* to be covered thoroughly are checked and run during the skeleton backfield drills. Work on hand-offs, placing the ball, and timing the plays can be worked out with a minimum loss of time. Again, every boy should work at top speed. We have had great success at Michigan State in having our boys hustle during the entire skeleton backfield work. If forty-five minutes are devoted to this drill, each boy should be pushed to his maximum on every play.

During the skeleton backfield drill, dummies can be brought into use to encourage better ball-handling and better running.

Spin plays

It would be good at this time to tie in the fundamentals described here with a practical situation, using our "124 play" as an illustration.

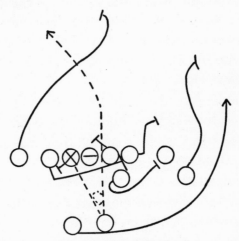

Fig. 53.   The "124 Play."

"124 play."   The left halfback in this play is directly behind the center with his eyes on the ball.   In learning our offense, left halfbacks feel often that because their eyes were straight forward in the "T" that they are not supposed to be watching the ball while

112

in this formation. Naturally, this is erroneous. The fullback splits the 4-5 man, and he too watches the ball. Either man is in a position to receive the ball on a direct snap from the center. The quarterback is stationed at the 3-4 seam versus an overshifted defense, and is directly behind the 4 man on an undershifted defense. This is to facilitate our ball-handling on the buck lateral series, which we will describe very shortly. In doing this we do not feel that we tip off the defense as to the type of play or to whether we are running right, left, or straight ahead. We have scouted ourselves in this respect and are satisfied that tips are not given. The right halfback is, as previously explained, 12 inches back and 12 inches out.

In building up our "124 play," the center should send the ball to the left knee of the fullback. The three-count pivot is made by the fullback. The left halfback, in taking his lead step, now should gain approximately six inches with his right foot, stepping to the toe of the fullback and placing his hands in a receiving position for the single wing exchange.

The fullback should place the ball into his stomach as quickly as possible and fake with his empty left hand by placing in the pocket of the left halfback. This synchronization should take place while the fullback is covering up the hole with his back. As he comes out of his spin, the ball should be wrapped high on the fullback's chest and his arms should cover the ball so that it cannot be seen. In the meantime, the left halfback must run an outside fake.

One of the greatest jobs of faking we have seen happened in the Penn State game of 1951 on a play similar to this. Bolden, our left halfback, ran a beautiful outside fake. He took one defending man with him and then, while continuing down the field, ended up in a position where he could break the ball carrier loose for a long touchdown run.

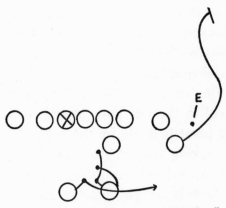

Fig. 54. The Pivots in the "124 Play."

The right halfback should fake a block on the end and, in so doing, get his attention and also catalog him for future use. He then runs for an inside position on the defensive halfback. The quarterback should start out to his right and take an inside position; then he can go to his blocking assignments. At times we ask the right halfback to run a reverse, calling this the *wing around*.

A companion play for the "124" is the "128" for the right halfback. Whether he carries the ball or not, his footwork should be such that he gains a great percentage of his depth on his first step. The reason for this is that as he passes the fullback, we do not want him going away from the formation or, as we call it, "sliding across the formation." Rather, we want him

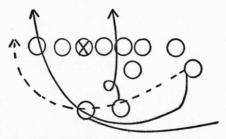

Fig. 55. The "128 Play" for the Right Halfback.

straightened out so that as he receives the ball on the reverse he is in a position to turn upfield and do the job that the assignment calls for.

"*114 play.*" The "114 play" is exactly the same play as the "124" as far as the line is concerned. The difference now is that the defense gets a different picture of the play. First, the ball is centered to the right knee of the fullback and the full spin is made to his right. The right half now does not have to gain as much ground because he receives the ball much sooner.

The left half and quarterback go to their left as diagrammed. Again the faking takes place so that the intent will be covered up from the defensive man involved.

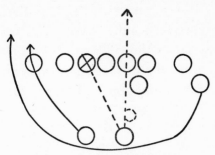

Fig. 56. The "114 Play." The line action is similar to that of the "124 play."

A principle that we have for crossing backs ("124 wing around") is that any time two backs cross, the left halfback is responsible for getting out of the way of the right halfback. We have found that this eliminates bumping. During the little that does occur, responsibility is quickly placed and corrections are made.

Buck lateral

When we use the buck lateral ("144"), a new teaching technique is involved. The ball is snapped to the center of the fullback's body. The quarterback is instructed to hop around in place with his back to the line and form a pocket on his right hip with the palms of each hand facing each other. The thumbs are pointed straight up in the air, and the fingers are straight forward. The fullback is instructed to place the ball into the quarterback's hands with the point straight forward. If he is faking, he merely puts the ball in and then pulls it out and continues on his way. The left halfback is instructed to do just the opposite

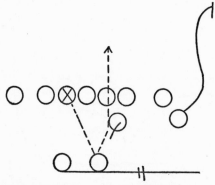

Fig. 57. The Buck Lateral "144 Play." Backs should lose ground *gradually*.

of what he does during the "124." He is asked to gain six inches on the "124" with his right foot and also to point it in toward the formation. Now he is asked to *lose* two yards while traveling ten.

We have found that our backs like to lose the two yards on the first step. This is absolutely wrong. The loss of two yards should be gradual. What we are trying to do is create a lateral position at the defensive end's position so that he has a big territory to cover.

On the buck lateral with the pitch-out, we ask our quarterbacks to use a spiral pass and to aim the ball at the letter of the left halfback. If fumbling occurs on the pitch-out, we have, in the past, numbered the footballs and have asked the receiver to tell us the number of the ball as he locks it into his hands.

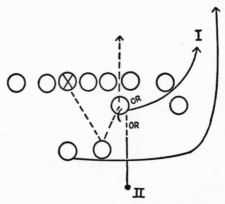

Fig. 58. The Buck Lateral with the Pitch-Out. The quarterback may duck into the off-tackle hole or go back and simulate a buck lateral pass.

Invariably the left half wishes to take off before he has the possession of the ball—thus creating the fumble. It should be pointed out that any time the ball is dropped on a buck lateral pass while on the pitch-out, it is interpreted as a fumble and can be recovered by either team.

The footwork of the quarterback after pitching the

ball out is of great concern to us. We instruct the quarterback to do one of two things. After pitching the ball out, he may duck into the off-tackle hole and become a blocker, or he may go back and simulate his buck lateral pass, which is a typical play used at Michigan State.

"Wedge play at 4"

Our "wedge play at 4" is a power play at 4. Here we try to pick out two defensive men and try to gain the desired yardage over them. The halfbacks do not enter into the faking picture too much because, as the name implies, this is a straight power wedge play; a quarterback is either false blocking or stepping into the hole as a blocker. This play has proved quite beneficial to us when meeting teams that drop linemen off, or against teams that loop or slant. This will be described more completely in the chapter covering the running offense.

"Left halfback at 4"

"Left halfback at 4" is a play with single-wing blocking. During this play we ask the right halfback and fullback to pivot and run a right-end sweep. The right halfback ends up by taking the inside position on the defensive left halfback while the fullback continues his sweep. From his square stance the quarterback uses a front pivot and makes a fake to the fullback who is running wide.

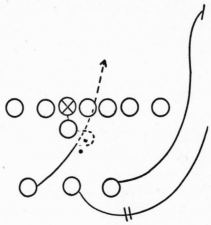

Fig. 59. "Left Halfback at 4."

During this fake, we ask the quarterback to make a 270-degree turn and hand the ball back to the left half-back who, after taking a slight position step with his right foot, runs through the 4-hole. As soon as the ball has been handed off, we ask the quarterback to pitch again to the fullback and then go back to his cup and fake a pass. At the same time, the quarterback is look-ing over the defense to find the reaction to his plays and ball-handling.

120

"Double wing at 4"

The "double wing at 4" is a fine play to tie in with the passing game and with the left halfback running an end sweep. On the "double wing fullback at 4," the quarterback makes a front pivot and hands the ball

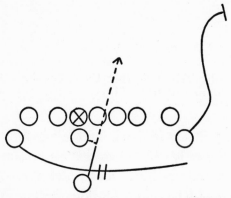

Fig. 60. The " 'T' Double Wing, Left Half at 4."
This is a good play to tie in with a passing game.

to the fullback who runs into the 4-hole. The left halfback comes around and accepts a fake from the quarterback who, after faking, goes back into his pass pattern and again catalogs the defense while checking to see the results of his faking.

"Left half up, fullback at 4"

The "left half up, fullback at 4" play is similar to the "double wing, fullback at 4" play as far as the footwork

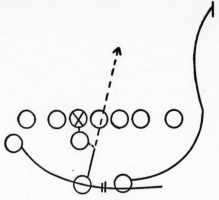

Fig. 61. The "Left Half Up, Fullback at 4."
This is similar to the "Double Wing, Fullback
at 4."

of the quarterback, fullback, and left halfback is concerned. The only change is that the right halfback
now runs directly at his defensive left end, and, after
slipping this end, he runs for inside position on the halfback.

6

Team Running
Offense

By now I am sure that you will agree that our running offense, although diversified and flexible, is not nearly as complicated as it might appear at first hand. By applying our simplified signal system to the various formations and by following clear-cut rules and principles, our men have comparatively few assignments to learn. We can hit either of our outside zones and over each of our offensive men in many different ways with little or no change in blocking assignments.

To show how our blocking rules and the signal system are used throughout our various formations, I would like to illustrate the number of plays we have hitting over our No. 4 man. Although there may be different ball-handling in the backfield or some minor change in the backfield technique, all of the plays have one thing in common: the same blocking at the line. We can hit over this No. 4 man fourteen different ways with the same blocking technique.

Fourteen plays with the same blocking

Since we started our offensive numbering by first taking up our single wing attack, I will start with a "24 play." This is a trap on the man playing head-on, or the first man to the outside of our No. 4 man. In this play the ball is passed to the fullback who spins and fakes to the left halfback, keeps the ball, and hits over the No. 4 man, who is the lead blocker, as diagrammed in Figure 62.

In the next instance, all we have done is to move the right halfback to an upwing position. Everyone else has the same position as the "24 play." When we

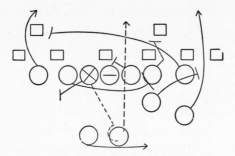

Fig. 62.   The "24 Play."

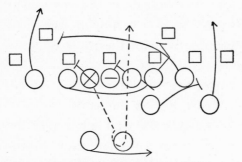

Fig. 63.   The "124 Play."

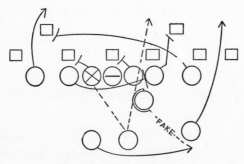

Fig. 64.   The "44 Play."

run it from this formation, the play is numbered "124" (see Figure 63).

We will use the same blocking from the buck lateral series, passing the ball to the fullback, who in turn will fake to the quarterback. The quarterback, on the snap of the ball, will hop around, and, after being faked the ball by the fullback, will in turn fake a pitch-out to the left halfback, who is running toward the 1-zone. The right halfback is in a deep wing position. This is called our "44 play" (see Figure 64).

Once again, by simply moving the wingback to an upwing position, we run the same play and call it a "144 play" (see Figure 65).

By reversing the assignments of the left halfback and the fullback, we hit the same hole with identical blocking by passing the ball directly to the left half-back, having him carry the ball into the line after fak ing to the quarterback. The fullback will run to the 1-zone and the quarterback fakes a pitch-out to the fullback. This is called a "44A play" (see Figure 66).

Once again we move the right halfback to an up-wing position and we have a "144A play" (see Figure 67).

All of the preceding four plays are run after shifting to the single wing and are begun on a single wing starting count. We can run a " 'T' 24 play" passing the ball directly through the quarterback's legs to the full-

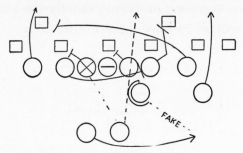

Fig. 65.   The "144 Play."

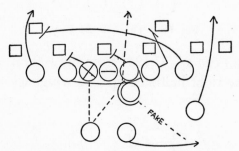

Fig. 66.   The "44A" Play.

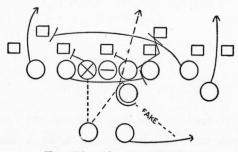

Fig. 67.   The "144A" Play.

127

back, with everyone executing exactly the same block as in a regular "24 play" (see Figure 68).

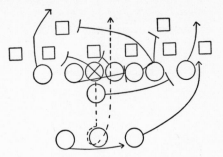

Fig. 68.   The " 'T' 24 Play."

We can run a " 'T' 124" from the 100 formation by having the right halfback up as a wingback (see Figure 69).

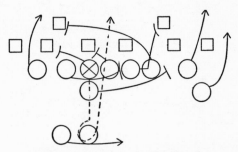

Fig. 69.   The " 'T' 124 Play."

We can, and do run this play off our buck lateral series from our "T" formation, with a direct pass through the quarterback's legs.   When the wingback is deep we call it a " 'T' 44 play" (see Figure 70).

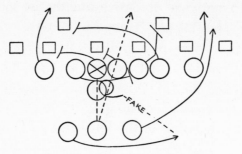

Fig. 70.   The "'T' 44 Play."

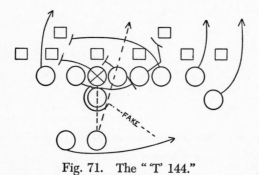

Fig. 71.   The "'T' 144."

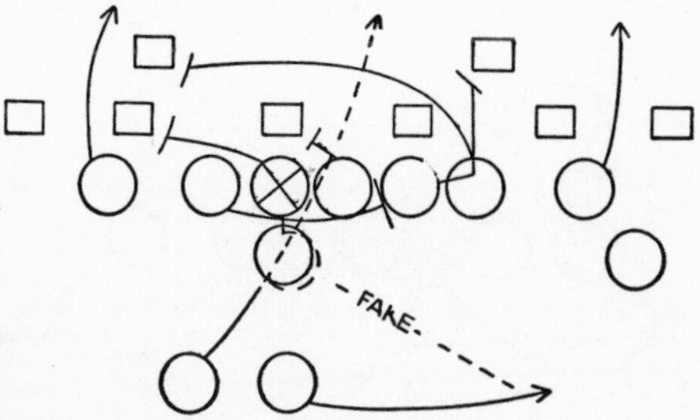

Fig. 72.   The "Left Half at 4."   This is a very
good ground-gaining play.

Then from our "T" 100 formation we run a " 'T' 144 play" (see Figure 71).

One of our very best ground-gaining plays the past few years has been "left half at 4." In this play we have retained the single-wing blocking principles but have the quarterback coming out to his right, pivoting around and handing to the left halfback, who slashes

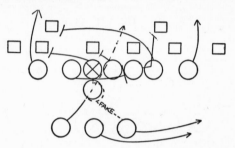

Fig. 73. The " 'T' 100, Left Half at 4."

over the No. 4 man with the right halfback and the full-back flaring (see Figure 72).

If we were to run this from our "T" 100 formation we would call it " 'T' 100, left half at 4" (see Figure 73).

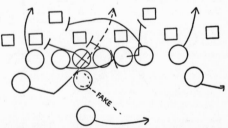

Fig. 74. The " 'T' Double Wing, Left Half at 4."

If we want to use the same blocking technique from our "T" double wing, we simply call it "'T' double wing, left half at 4" (see Figure 74).

And, finally, we will use this technique from our latest formation, which has the left half up, and simply call it "left half up, left half at 4" (see Figure 75).

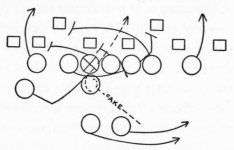

Fig. 75. The "Left Half Up, Left Half at 4."

You may question the advantages of running so many different ways with the same simplified blocking rules. I will try to give a full and meaningful explanation in the succeeding paragraphs.

Confronting the defense

One of the biggest problems facing any running offense in present-day football is the number of different defensive formations that are being used against them. The question that we hear most often from fellow coaches throughout the country is "How do you cope with changing defenses?"

To my mind there are two types of changing defenses—those that present varying alignments before the snap of the ball, and those that change after the snap of the ball by using devices such as slanting, crosscharging, looping, or plugging.

As a staff, we are convinced that the biggest strength of our offense is our ability to run any of our plays against any conceivable type of defense. Naturally, it is true that certain plays will function much better against one defense than another, principally because some defenses present more difficult blocking angles for the offensive men. But we feel that if our men will follow their principles that we can call any play in our offense in the huddle and have a good chance of running it successfully, regardless of the defense that may confront it.

In the first chapter of this book I pointed out to you that teams were defensing our formations by placing their defensive strength to meet our offensive strength—a basically sound idea—with the result that we weren't able to move the ball as well as we would have liked to. We feel that we have, for the most part, eliminated the problem of not knowing what defense we were going to face by getting the opposition to show their hand as early in the ball game as possible. We don't feel that any one team can adequately prepare and execute more than a single defense for each of our offensive formations. To a casual observer it may look as though we are picking plays and formations out of a hat, and, quite frankly, there are times that this would be a good definition of what we are trying to do.

Once we find how a team will defense our "T" 100, our "T," our "T" double wing, our left half up, our deep single wing, and our up single wing—and can find what we feel is a weak spot in two or three of these defenses—we will have an offensive advantage. As a result, we will immediately start limiting our attack to take advantage of these defensive weaknesses of the opposing team.

We may find, for example, that a team is giving us the strong-side flank from our single wing and thereby give us the opportunity to gain ground on a 121 sweep play. The defense they are using against our "T" formation gives our No. 7 and 8 men good cross-blocking angles, making "right half at 8" very effective against that defense.

It is possible that the same team may defense our "T" double wing by using a five-man line with no middle linebacker, dropping him back with the expectation that we are going to pass from this formation. We might have a very good opening and would run a " 'T' double wing, full-back at 5 trap" up the middle. Once we have determined that we can make ground from these various formations, we will keep concentrating on these few plays until the defense makes some adjustment to stop us. However, in so doing they will probably leave a weakness at some other spot along the line.

The running attack

I don't want to give the impression that it is an easy matter for our offense, or any offense, to gain a lot of ground from a running attack by the simple device of using multiple formations. Nothing could be further from the truth. There is absolutely no substitute for good, hard shoulder blocking in any running attack.

If I were to list the two main factors in any success we have had as a running team, they would be: first, good shoulder blocking; and second, excellent team take-off. We have geared our offense to a fast take-off. To me, team speed is much more important than individual speed. It would certainly be better to have 11 boys of average speed take off together than to have 11 "ten-second" men in your lineup and have them start spasmodically.

Almost half of our entire practice time is spent with our offensive men pounding the dummies in a full-speed signal session. This accomplishes quite a few things. It perfects the timing of offensive plays, it enables your entire team to get the feeling that every play has to be run at top speed whether in practice or in a game, and it develops hardness among your blockers by having them pound the dummies relentlessly. The men who hold the dummies put a lot of pressure behind them to simulate, as much as possible, a live defensive man.

These continuous dummy scrimmages have developed our team speed more than any single part of our practice sessions. My definition of team speed would be *eleven men hitting simultaneously as quickly as possible.*

Against changing defenses

When we are confronted with the type of defenses that change after the snap of the ball, such as cross-charges, stunting, or looping, we like to run quick-hitting plays and try to catch defensive linemen out of position and prevent them from recovering. We will often concentrate on the 1- and 9-zones and over the No. 2 and 8 men against stunting defenses, because these spots are most often left vulnerable when the defense is juggling its personnel around.

Another means we have of taking advantage of stunting linemen is by the use of wedge plays, especially in a short yardage situation. We have been very successful with this type of attack.

Position of offensive players

Even though I do feel that good blocking and team speed are the first requisites in having a good running game, there is no question in my mind about the help that the deployment of our offensive men in different formations has given us in achieving better blocking angles, which is the ultimate aim of any good offense. If we can cause the defense to make adjustments to meet our various methods of attack, there is more chance for them to leave an area unguarded where we will be able to get good blocking angles on two adjacent defensive men and thus enable us to gain a lot of ground.

Just as in any other offense, there are certain plays that can be used more advantageously on certain parts of the field. For example, "left half at 4" is a very good play off the left strip, and, inversely, "right half at 6" is very good off the right strip. I will cover this in more detail in a later chapter when discussing quarterback strategy.

Other factors in the running game

In addition to the defenses used against us, there are other factors that influence our selection of plays and formations during the course of a ball game.

Using the personnel efficiently. We feel that we can best utilize our personnel by running them on the type of plays for which they are most physically suited. When we are using small fast scatbacks, we try to use plays that hit just as quickly as possible. We can do this by utilizing a lot of our straight "T" attack. We can use our power runners usually to better advantage by having them run our single-wing power plays with double-team blocking at the hole.

A good running back is valuable at any one of three backfield positions. If by chance we happen to have two left halfbacks that are both better runners than any of our fullbacks or right halfbacks, we can move one to another position and get the maximum use out of our personnel. It is an ideal situation to have your good running backs also be good blockers, but this is not always the case, so it helps to have a variety of offensive plays that can be run efficiently with some backs who are not necessarily expert blockers.

The quarterback. To carry this idea of proper utilization further, probably the best example is to be found at the quarterback position in our offense. To be able to handle all of the duties we ask of our quarterback in our various formations, a young man has to have superior ability and excellent reflexes. We would like to have him be a good ball handler, a good passer, runner, blocker, and signal-caller. However, it is almost impossible to find this combination. It is

137

a rare occasion when you have one individual who possesses all of these qualifications.

It is often necessary to have two or more boys to combine all of the skills that are so necessary in the successful operation of the multiple offense. To illustrate, we might have one quarterback who is a fine passer and good ball handler. These two abilities seem to go hand in hand. We can have him run our "T" single wing offense with the ball passed through his legs and have a lineman execute the difficult primary block usually executed by the quarterback in a conventional single wing. In order not to become stereotyped as a straight "T" quarterback, he can shift to the single wing and run the buck lateral series in which he still remains primarily a ball handler or a faker. We may have another quarterback on the squad not quite as adept at ball-handling and passing but who is a rugged blocker. It is only natural that he will lean more to the single wing offense where he will retain the key blocking assignments that a single wing quarterback is usually called upon to perform.

Environment. It may seem surprising, but the climate and the geographical location of your school have a direct bearing on the amount of time you should spend in perfecting a running attack. When you are coaching in a section of the country where the weather is, at best, uncertain, and rainy Saturday afternoons are commonplace—and upon occasion snow storms and blizzards are not out of the question—it would be foolhardy not to have the strongest running attack that you can possibly muster. On the other hand, if you are in a section of the country where the climate has a case history of providing dry and fair game days, it is quite possible that you will want to rely less on your running attack and stress your passing offense. I don't want to give the impression that because Michigan State is located in the north, where there are days not conducive to an aerial attack, we pass only out of desperation.

In 1951, Al Dorow, our fine quarterback of that season, established an all-time Michigan State passing record, both in number of completions and total yards gained. In the following season of 1952, Tom Yewcic, a young man who stepped into Dorow's shoes, surpassed Dorow's records. There is no question about the tremendous aid that our passing game received by the threat of a strong running attack.

Team unity

A very important factor in the success we have had as a running team has been the supreme confidence our boys have in our signal system and in our complete offense. They have learned to believe sincerely that any play called by the quarterback has a reasonable chance of succeeding in gaining yardage. For a team, this matter of building up confidence in the offense cannot be stressed too much.

I am *not* referring, however, to the building up of a false sense of optimism by having your best boys run roughshod over a weak defensive group. They must believe and know that they can go against the very toughest of opposition—provided they carry out their assignments in a decent manner. Naturally, you want your boys to have this confidence in *all* of your offensive plays, which they can and will have, but as the season progresses they will have a few clutch plays psychologically speaking, which will rate highest in their estimation as a team. These are the "bread-and-butter" plays that the boys will run to perfection when some yardage is needed at a crucial point in a tough ball game. I try to augment this idea by giving them graphic and visual demonstrations by using movies, showing them *why* these particular plays have been so successful.

Shifting from right to left formation

Although for the most part we have been running from an unbalanced right formation, we occasionally will shift our unbalanced line to the left and run any play in our offense. Owing to the fact that we have our linemen take the same relative position in left formation as they do when they are unbalanced to the right, we can run our complete offense without the necessity of any of our men learning new assignments. It is simply a matter of the linemen blocking with the opposite shoulder, our fullbacks spinning in the opposite direction on spin plays, and so on.

Whenever we have a right halfback who runs exceptionally well to his left and is a better than average passer, we like to have him at the tailback position in our left formation to make the most out of his capabilities. Running from left formation also gives the opponents another defensive problem because it is impossible for them to know just what phase of offense we will run. Therefore, they have to try to prepare their defensive men for any eventuality.

When you take our complete offense from right formation and realize that, theoretically, we can double this by shifting left, you can see that the possibilities from our offense are certainly unlimited, both as to the type and the number of different plays we can run. However, we realize that it isn't possible to perfect this entire offense and run each play with the timing and precision that one is always striving for in coaching, so we make it a policy to concentrate always on a limited part of our offense for each game, stressing the plays we feel will be most effective against our coming opponent. On the other hand, we can and will utilize any play in our offense if an opening presents itself.

Although I discuss the running game and the passing game in different chapters, insofar as actual operation we consider them as one in our total offense, with one always aiding and abetting the other. I am sure that after you read the next chapter, on passing, you will see that at Michigan State running and passing are indivisible.

7

The Passing Game

To operate with success against the highly developed defenses of modern football, a team must achieve fine balance between the running and the passing game. Each of these important phases of offensive football should supplement the other. How much the passing attack should be emphasized in any one season depends, of course, on the ability of the available personnel.

To have a successful passing attack, it is necessary for coaches and quarterbacks to think of the pass as equal in importance to the running play. It must not be considered a weapon to be used as a last resort, or a third-down or long-yardage choice. Modern strategy demands the use of passing in the first and second down, with increasingly less restriction imposed by field position.

A well-rounded pass offense must be equipped to meet the great variety of situations created by the numerous types of pass defense, individual defensive weaknesses, unusually hard rushing, and the necessity of making some passes look exactly like running plays.

Since we operate our running game from a number of offensive formations, it is necessary to be able to pass from all of these formations. Some coaches insist that every pass be made to look like one of the running plays, while others use the simple drop-back method of passing to good advantage.

I think there are merits to both ways, and we try to incorporate both into our passing game. Logically, we want our best passer to do most of our passing, and in order to have him throw from all our formations certain adjustments are necessary. The different ways of achieving this are indicated in the passing diagrams that follow. However, it is necessary to have other backs throw the ball occasionally to keep the defense honest on some of our best running plays.

Calling passes

Our method of calling pass plays has been mentioned briefly in Chapter 2. We indicate the number one receiver and the lane he should take, prefacing this information with the technique or formation from which we want the pass thrown. For example: spin pass, left end cross; buck lateral, left half flat; "T" 100, right half cross. Those which closely resemble running plays are given the name of the play—"41 pass," "131 running pass," "21 pass to the quarterback." To those passes that are rather special in nature we give special names, for instance, "41 transcontinental to the quarterback."

The diagram illustrates the terms that describe the lanes we want the number one receivers to take. These lanes apply equally to the right end and to any back who is close to the line of scrimmage. Most of them also apply to any back who is in a deeper position. The majority of these lanes are self-explanatory, but I will comment on several of them that may need clarification.

The spot pass is received on the run, and is the shortest, quickest pass we throw. The stop pattern is a hook pass on which the receiver runs right at a defensive man who has been retreating quickly. The word "stop" distinguishes it from the regular hook pattern, on which the receiver goes straight downfield from his position to a depth of about eight yards. On a stop pass the receiver might go as far as twelve or fifteen yards before hooking.

On patterns like out, in, away, and deep, the receiver always tries to use some kind of fake on the defensive man before breaking to the indicated lane. On the hook pattern we can fake a pass to the receiver

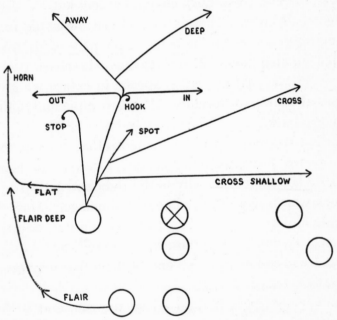

Fig. 76. Lanes for Pass Receivers. Each line represents the direction a receiver may take.

and then have him go to any of the four lanes mentioned above. In other words, we can have a left end hook-and-out pattern, or a left end hook-and-deep. On the horn pattern the receiver, while he is running in the flat, looks at the passer. The passer fakes to him, preferably with a full arm movement. At this signal the receiver turns and looks for the ball over his inside shoulder.

In addition to the usual patterns, a back starting from a fairly deep position is often run on the *flare* or the *flare* deep lanes, as illustrated in Figure 76.

The flexibility of this method of calling passes is very obvious. It is entirely possible to use spur-of-the-moment passes during the game without causing too much confusion to the passer or the receivers.

Types of passes

When the lane of the number one receiver has been indicated, the decoys on that particular pass pattern must recognize instantly the lanes they must take in order to clear the number one receiver. In the pass shown in Figure 77, the right end knows that he must run through the safety man, and the right halfback must decoy the defensive halfback toward the sideline.

In building a passing attack we try to anticipate defense situations and then prepare to meet them. We work from our short patterns to the longer ones.

We must be able to put a receiver in any open area, take advantage of any poor defender, and make the best possible use of our own personnel. The double

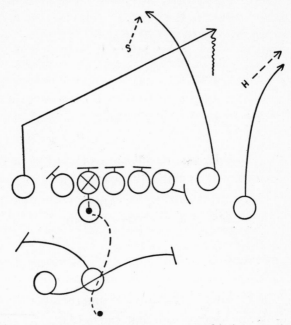

Fig. 77.   With the left end as the number one receiver, decoys run through the safety man and draw the defensive right half toward the sideline.

flare, right end hook is an example of a pass that tests the defensive responsibility of a linebacker.

The spot pattern puts receivers quickly into areas uncovered by linebackers. It is the responsibility of the receiver to avoid interception. He should never

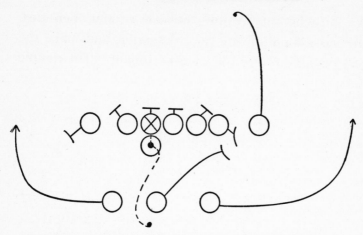

Fig. 78. "Double Flare, Right End Hook." This is a pass play which exploits poor defensive backs.

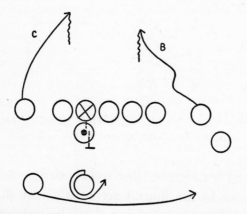

Fig. 79. Spot Pass to the Left or Right End. It is the receiver's responsibility to avoid interception.

149

ask the passer to throw through a linebacker. This pass is automatic with us. We use it against plugging linebackers, as well as to take quick advantage of a close exposed area.

The next pass is the type that permits us to put a fast man against a defender who may not be able to match his speed (see Figure 80).

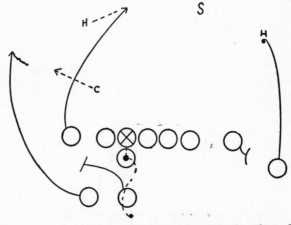

Fig. 80. The "'T' 100, Left Half Flare." This play utilizes a fast back against a slow defender.

Against a plugging linebacker, or one who plays rather close to the line of scrimmage, the jump pass from buck lateral series and the fake dive pass from the "T" have been very successful.

On our short, quick passes our linemen fire out on protection.

150

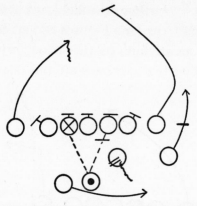

Fig. 81. The Jump Pass from Buck Lateral Series. This play is useful against aggressive linebackers.

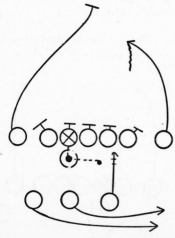

Fig. 82. A fake to the right half and a jump pass to the left end. This is another useful pass play against a plugging linebacker.

151

Moving a bit farther downfield, we have the hooks and the out patterns (see Figures 83 and 84).

Some passes are built on the "flood" principle. By this I mean that two receivers are put against one de-

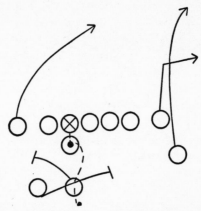

Fig. 83. The "T" 100, Right End Out." This is another play in which the quarterback passes.

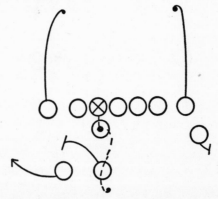

Fig. 84. The "T" 100, Left End Hook."

fender, or three receivers against two defenders. An example of this type of pass is shown in Figure 85, and I am going to take time here to show how this pass may be thrown from each of our formations. I will indi-

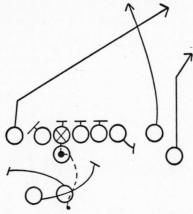

Fig. 85. Using the "Flood" Principle: *1*. The " 'T' 100, Left End Cross."

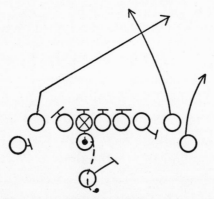

Fig. 86. Using the "Flood" Principle: *2*. The " 'T' 200, Left End Cross."

cate slight adjustments in protection that are necessary.

To take advantage of superior personnel we must include a type of pass that isolates a defender and allows a receiver to run an individual or personal pattern.   This is illustrated in Figure 89.

We want to be sure to include some passes that tie in with our best running plays.

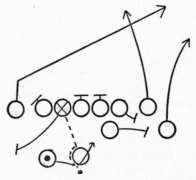

Fig. 87.   Using the "Flood" Principle:
3. The "Spin Pass, Left End Cross."

There are several means by which a passing attack may overcome unusually hard rushing, and obviously one way would be to get rid of the ball quickly (as seen on some of the short passes already illustrated).   Another popular method is to throw the screen passes. The fake pass and run or the draw play are effective against hard rushing.   To throw deeper patterns, it is almost necessary to throw running passes or, if operat-

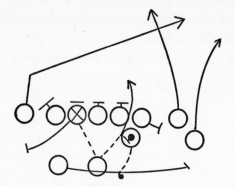

Fig. 88. Using the "Flood" Principle: *4.*
The "Buck Lateral, Left End Cross."

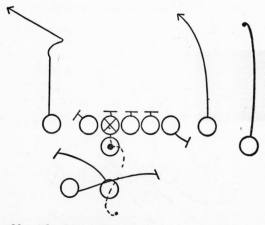

Fig. 89. The "T" 100, Left End In and Away. The
right half is a flanker. This pass takes advantage of
the superiority of one player.

155

ing from the "T," a roll-out pass by the quarterback. A screen, a draw play, and a roll-out pass are seen in Figures 94, 95, and 96.

Another situation that we meet rather frequently is

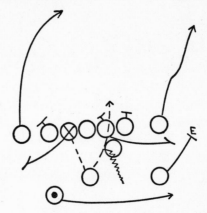

Fig. 90. The "41 Pass." This pass ties in with a running play.

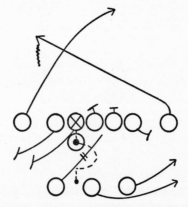

Fig. 91. The "Left Half at 4 Pass." This pass is related to a running play.

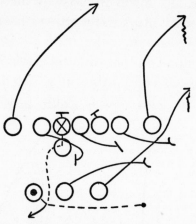

Fig. 92. The "Left Half at 1 Sweep Pass." This is similar to one of the better running plays.

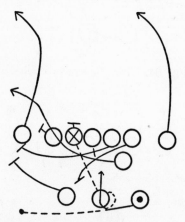

Fig. 93. The "19 Pass." This pass also resembles one of the best running plays.

157

the double safety found in the 5-4-2 and 6-3-2 defensive alignments. An obvious answer to these defenses is the type of pass demonstrated in Figure 97.

In developing our passing game through the course of the season we constantly add, revise, and eliminate pass patterns. There is a tendency sometimes to add

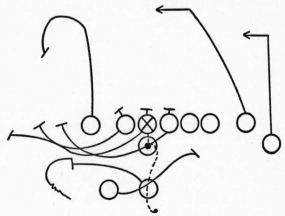

Fig. 94. The "Screen to Fullback."

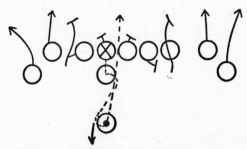

Fig. 95. The "Draw to Fullback." This is another screen pass.

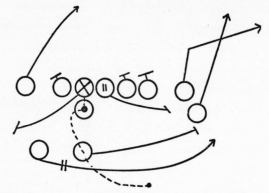

Fig. 96. The "T" 100 Roll-Out." The right end is out.

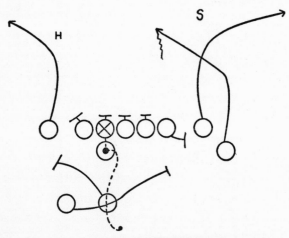

Fig. 97. The "T" 100, Right Half Cross." This is used against a double-safety defense.

too many patterns, but we try to have a good reason for our new ones. These decisions are based partly on scouting reports and partly on logical sequences to the patterns and running plays that have been successful for us in previous games.

In illustrating these various passes I have tried to indicate how easy it is to take advantage of exceptional passing ability of players in any of the backfield positions.

Pass protection

The type of blocking that we use on pass protection has been described already in a previous chapter. I do want to emphasize here that we spend a tremendous amount of time in an attempt to get the very best protection for our passer that we can.

We caution the passer to cover his passes, particularly those thrown to a flank. In addition, we ask those men who form the outside part of our protection to accept a coverage responsibility also. For instance, in Figure 98 our fullback and left halfback are the outside men in the protection, and in this particular pass our fullback should recognize the importance of getting on out after his protection block in order to cover the possibility of an interception.

We encourage the passer to time his delivery to anticipate the point at which the receiver will break into the clear. Passes thrown too late end in interceptions.

One mark of a great passer is that he suffers few interceptions. He must take advantage of his protection and stay in the pocket on certain passes right

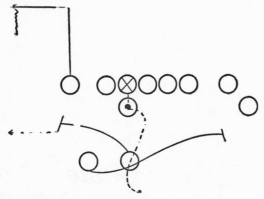

Fig. 98. The "'T' 100, Left End Out." The fullback is an outside man and should cover the possibility of an interception.

up to the last moment. If he has to keep the ball and run with it, we hope he will make every effort to get back up to the line of scrimmage, at least, avoiding the temptation to circle back and take a chance on losing so much yardage that the whole complexion of the situation is changed.

8

The Kicking Game as an Offensive Weapon

It is natural for people to think of a kick in football as a defensive measure; however, we are convinced that a finely developed kicking game is one of the greatest offensive weapons in football. Undoubtedly the outcome of more football games is vitally affected by the successful or unsuccessful exploitation of the kicking game than by any other department of football.

Kicking formations

Let's start our discussion of the kicking game with the punt.   There are three popular methods of executing this maneuver in present-day football:

1. The closed punt formation
2. Spread kick formation
3. Quick-kick formation

The closed punt formation.   The closed punt formation is designed to give adequate protection to the kicker by forming a cup and preventing any defensive man from getting to a point where he can prevent the kicker from getting the ball away successfully. This is a balanced line formation with only the right end split off, providing the protection is for a right-footed kicker.   The right end in this case is not needed for protection because we have two backfield men protecting the side of the kicker's foot.   The left end, on occasion, may also split off to be in a better position to cover the kick but will move in next to his companion tackle if there is a recognized attempt being made to block a kick on his side of the line.

In protecting for a punt from this formation, we have our center pass the ball and then chuck back and remain solid to prevent himself from being pulled. The guards have one responsibility, namely, to protect their inside seam or the space between themselves and the center. They do this by anchoring their outside foot and taking a short step to the inside with the foot nearest the center.

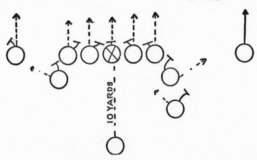

Fig. 99. Closed Punt Formation and Coverage.

The sole responsibility of the tackles is to protect the seam between themselves and their offensive guards. They follow the same principle of anchoring their outside foot and taking a short step to the inside with the foot nearest their companion guard. We will line two backs up a little to the outside and a yard behind their offensive tackles, splitting the outside leg of the offensive tackle. Their first responsibility is to allow no one to come between them and the offensive tackle, so their first movement is to step with their inside foot toward the tackle and to be absolutely certain that there is no one coming to their inside before they bump anyone trying to go around them. The remaining back would also protect on the right in the case of a right-footed kicker and would be a yard back and splitting the outside leg of the back in front of him, with the responsibility of protecting the seam between himself and the front back. He, too, steps with his inside foot.

The kicker lines up at ten yards from the center, and in the case of a two-step kicker, the ball will leave his foot at a spot approximately six yards behind the line of scrimmage. Thus, it is imperative that no defensive man be permitted to get into the path of the flight of the ball.

This formation gives fine protection but does not lend itself to rapid kick coverage. In covering from this formation we will always release the right end on the snap of the ball and will do the same with the left end, providing the defense is not loading up his area and trying to block the punt from that side of the line of scrimmage. The remaining linemen will protect their inside seam and will not release until they hear the kicker's foot meet the ball. When they do start downfield, we stress that kicks be covered with tremendous speed.

We feel that one of the most important points in coverage is not to have one man follow downfield in another's footsteps when one good block may erase both men. We want them to fan out so that they can cover all sections of the field. The two front backs will fan out to the right and left and become defensive halfbacks. The deep protecting back on the side of the kicker's foot will cover down the middle, and the kicker will become a safety man in our coverage (see Figure 99).

The spread kick formation. In order to get faster coverage of punts and to cut down the effectiveness of the organized punt return, which has become a potent weapon in recent years, a great many teams have been utilizing a spread punt formation. In this formation linemen are split off so that a wider area can be covered going down the field under punts. In most spread punt formations, the linemen release immediately or simply bump and go upon the snap of the ball. Because the protection of the kicker is sacrificed, he is placed at a depth of fourteen yards from the center to enable him to have more time to get the kick away.

We kick, on occasions, from a spread kick formation, and I will give you the simple rules that we try to follow. We give our center one responsibility and that is to pass the ball 14 yards back to the kicker with as much speed as possible. If there is a man on him, he bumps him and then heads downfield. If there is no defensive man on him, he releases immediately.

We have our guards split off two yards from the center. They block the man to their outside and disregard anyone playing head on them. They will hit hard without holding their blocks and then release and start downfield to cover the kick. The tackles are split three yards from their companion guards and release immediately upon the snap of the ball. When there is a man on them they try to avoid him and get downfield as soon as possible.

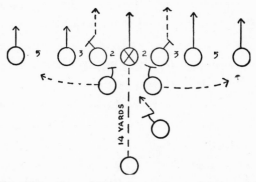

Fig. 100.   Spread Punt Formation and Coverage.

The ends are split off at least five yards from their tackles and they too will cover the kick as soon as the ball is snapped. We have two of our backs in the seams between the guards and the center at a depth of two yards. They will step with their inside foot and block the first man coming through to their outside. The remaining protecting back is placed at a depth of seven yards and is a free blocker, who may block anyone who is apt to get in the path of the flight of the ball.

We try to keep our principles of coverage pretty much the same in both of these formations. We have the two front backs fan out and become the defensive halfbacks just as we do in our closed punt formation. The deep defensive back covers the punt formation going down the middle.

Our choice of formations to kick from would depend a lot on the personnel in the ball game and on our position on the field. Naturally, we would not attempt to kick from a spread punt formation unless we had a center in the ball game who could pass the ball the 14 yards back to the kicker with a fair amount of speed. When we have to kick from deep in our own territory we prefer to use the closed kick formation to insure getting the ball away. The spread formation is shown in Figure 100.

Quick-kick formation. The quick-kick formation relies upon the element of surprise for its effectiveness, so naturally it is used only on a first, second, or third down, and never on a fourth down or an obvious fourth-down kicking situation. This maneuver is executed from our single wing back formation with an unbalanced line. The protection is necessarily quite different from that of a regular punt formation.

We have our right tackle and outside guard, the No. 3 and 4 men respectively, pair off and kick out shoulder to shoulder. We have the inside guard and center, or the No. 5 and 6 men respectively, pairing off and kicking out; the No. 7 man blocks the man on him or the first man to his outside; and the quarterback blocks out the first man outside of his own right tackle. The fullback will allow the ball to pass in front of him to the left halfback and will cross over and block the first man outside of his No. 7 man or left tackle. We

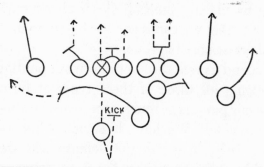

Fig. 101. Quick-Kick Formation and Coverage.

quick-kick on a fairly long count to enable our kicker to start back a couple of counts before the snap of the ball. This gives him enough depth when he catches the ball so that he can start his kicking motion just as soon as it reaches his hands. We have a very fine running series from this quick-kick formation that I will discuss in more detail later on in this chapter.

We will punt or quick-kick the ball for various reasons. Naturally, we will punt on fourth down with long yardage in order to get the ball away from our own goal.   We will often quick-kick when we have the wind at our back to gain yardage more readily than we might possibly do from some other play.   When we have a good accurate punter we will often kick even though we have possession of the ball in our opponent's territory, if we feel that he can place the ball out of bounds outside of the 20-yard line.   In all of these cases we have one thought in mind, and that is to gain yardage by placing the ball closer to our opponent's goal line so that we can repossess it and go in to score in the shortest possible time.

We spend a great deal of time on our punting game in practicing all three of these types of formations. We give our punters as much experience kicking under fire as possible.   We have live-contact practice sessions regularly, in which the defense will use every imaginable stunt to try to put heat on the kicker, blocking the punt whenever possible.

There are a few coaching points that I try to get across that relate to the individual formations.   I have one axiom for all of our punters when kicking from a regular punt formation, and that is, *"Either kick the ball high or out of bounds."*   The reason for this is quite obvious.   When the ball is kicked high it gives the men covering more time to get downfield after the ball.   If it is kicked out of bounds, height is of no consequence because the ball cannot be returned.

When we kick from a spread formation, we want

to keep the ball in the field of play so that we will have an opportunity to benefit by any rolling of the ball if it is not fielded by the receiving team. In quick-kicking, we like to have the ball kicked low so that it will hit and bounce, and not give the safety man time to get back and field it.

We spend as much time in the preparation of returning our opponent's kicks as we do in our various punt formations. We will use several methods of returning punts. Some will involve a double safety with a criss-cross or a fake hand-off, while at other times we will use one deep man returning the ball.

If a punt by our opponents is virtually assured by the down yardage and position on the field, we will always have an organized punt return and will plan to return the ball either right, left, or middle. When we are returning to the right or left, we will designate the linemen on the side where we are returning the ball as holding men, and the men on the opposite side as rushing men.

The rushing men put the pressure on the kicker and try to block the kick. Then they circle deep on the side where the kick is being returned and attempt to get an outside position on the men from the kicking team going downfield.

The linemen on the holding side will try to draw the block of the linemen or backs on that side to hold them there as long as possible, and then he will circle shallow. A return of this nature requires a lot of timing and practice because the blockers must all get outside positions and the blocks must be put on at the right moment.

If a kick is to be returned to the right and the ball goes to the back on that side, he will carry it toward the middle of the field and will hand off to the other safety man who will return the ball to his right. If the ball

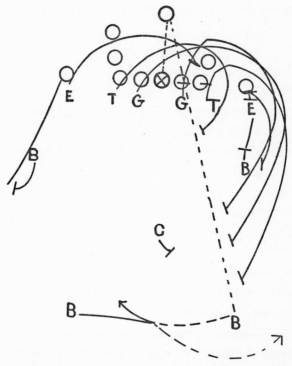

Fig. 102. Punt Return Right with a Double Safety.

is kicked to the safety man on the left side of the field, he will fake a hand-off to the safety man on the right. Exactly the opposite of this procedure would be employed if the return is on the left.

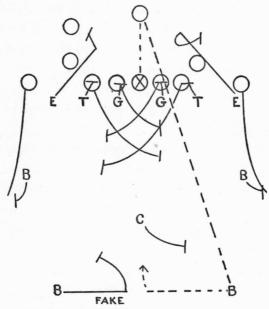

Fig. 103. The Middle Punt Return with a Double Safety.

In the criss-cross, the man with the ball always goes on the inside. The end on the holding side, or the side where the kick is to be returned, will try to block the offensive end at the line of scrimmage. The half-back on that side will also be assigned to the end, and

173

these two men will make repeated attempts to block this offensive man until they are successful in knocking him down or keeping him out of the play. The halfback on the opposite side will be responsible for the end on his side. The defensive center will drop back to a point approximately 20 yards behind the line of scrimmage and, when the ball is punted, will go back and protect the two safety men when they are making their criss-cross or exchanging the ball. He will block the most dangerous onrushing linemen. Figure 103 shows this punt return and the assignment of each defensive man.

It is possible to have the same return with a single safety by having your safety man field the ball and head upfield and then swing to right or left, depending on the return that has been called. When using this technique, we block the ends out and have the return go up inside of them.

Another type of punt return that we use, also with an option of having a double or single safety, is what we call a *middle return.* When we use a double safety we will fake a criss-cross and then have the man with the ball break up the field. Here, again, we attempt to block the ends out and will have our linemen cross-block as diagrammed.

When returning from a spread punt formation we will use various devices. Often we will try to block their men at the line of scrimmage and then put on a delayed circling return, having the back who fields the ball head upfield and break right or left and pick up the circling blockers. If the kick is high and the on-rushing linemen are downfield approximately the same

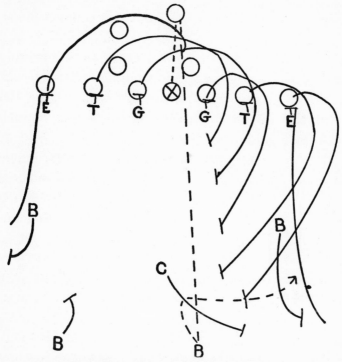

Fig. 104. The Spread Kick Return.

time that the ball is, we instruct our backs to signal for a fair catch to eliminate the roll of the ball.

We have found that probably the most effective weapon against a spread kick formation is to put a lot of heat on the kicker and force him to hurry his kick, which will usually cut down his distance and occasionally result in the blocking of a punt. The return against a spread kick is seen in Figure 104.

Kickoffs

Most of the time we will kick off in an orthodox manner by placing the ball in an upright position on a kickoff tee in the center of the field with five men on either side of the kicker.

In placing our men on a kickoff formation we like to have our ends play their normal positions as end men on the line because they are accustomed to being

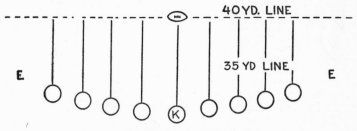

Fig. 105. The Kick-Off Formation.

in that position. The rest of our personnel will be placed regardless of their regular position. The sole determining factor will be their ability to get the job done at the spot where we place them. We like to have fast, rugged boys who are good tacklers next to the kicker because they will usually be the first men to get to the ball or the ball carrier, or at least to the opposing team's protective blockers, and the job that they perform will determine, to a large degree, the success that we have in preventing any long run-backs of kickoffs.

We will designate two second-wave men who may be the second or third men in from the sides. We change this from week to week. We call them second-wave men because they cover the kickoffs slower than the rest of the team; their job is to insure against any long touchdown runs. They are also in a position to cut off the ball carrier if he breaks through our first wave of coverage.

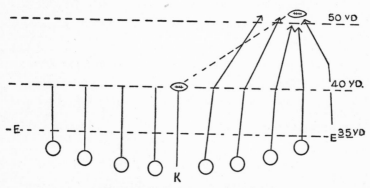

Fig. 106. The On-Side Kick.

When we have a good kickoff man we like to kick the ball high down the middle and rely on a speedy coverage to prevent run-backs. When we don't happen to be blessed with a superior kickoff man, we will sometimes resort to squibbing. We will simply place the ball flat on the tee with the points at a 45-degree angle to the goal posts. This type of kick is harder to handle, and we hope that any loss of distance will be made up by the inability of the receiving team to return the kick any great distance.

In kicking off we have our ends place their hands on their knees and take a position on the 35-yard line. They face in toward the kicker. The rest of the men are staggered and each man to the inside is a little deeper so that his line of vision to the kicker is unobstructed. As they get even with the kicker, they can move forward with him (see Figure 105).

Any time that the ball travels ten yards on a kick-off, it is a free ball and belongs to the team making the recovery. There have been games decided by this factor when teams have executed an onside kick successfully. We always practice this maneuver because we never know when it will be necessary for us to try to gain possession of the ball when trying to come from behind during the closing seconds of a ball game.

There are many methods of executing an onside kick, but probably one of the simplest and most effective is to have the kicker disguise his intentions right up to the last second. Then he kicks the ball to his right or left; the men on that side have been alerted and are ready to try to gain possession after the ball has gone ten yards (see Figure 106).

Kickoff returns

Well-organized kickoff returns became necessary years ago when the old "flying wedge" was outlawed by a rule making it mandatory for at least five men to be within fifteen yards of the ball when it is kicked. It is permissible to use these five men as blockers,

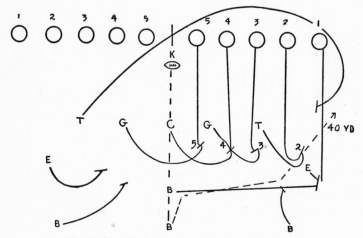

Fig. 107. The Side Line Kick-Off Return.

but they cannot cross this fifteen-yard restraining line until after the ball has been kicked.

We return kicks to either side or up the middle. The main coaching point in returns of this nature concerns the protection of the back until he gets into the slot that is being cleared for him. Most kickoff returns are predicated on splitting two of the covering men and then isolating the rest of the kicking team. Too often the key or primary blocks will be effective, but some member of the kicking team will close in from the side and tackle the ball carrier before he gets into the alley that has been cleared for him.

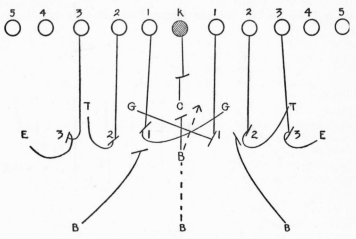

Fig. 108.   The Middle Kick-Off Return.

We use three deep backs.   If the ball goes to the middle back, the other two protect him and get him into the lane that we are attempting to clear for his return.   If the ball goes to one of the backs on the side, the middle back will take his place and protect him from that side.   The return to the side is seen in Figure 107, and the middle return is shown in Figure 108.

Field goals and extra points

We have made great use of the field goal as an offensive scoring weapon, and it has been the deciding factor in several of our ball games. In kicking field goals or extra points, the holder will spot the ball seven yards from the line of scrimmage. Our protection will be the same as for punts, except that our two protecting backfield men will be outside of their ends and a yard back and will protect the seam between themselves and the end.

The only distinction we make between a field goal attempt and an extra point is the matter of coverage—a field goal can be returned just like a punt—so we want our men covering on a field-goal attempt as long as the ball belongs in the field of play.

Countless games have been decided by the narrow margin of an extra point or a field goal. Too much time cannot be spent in this department of the game. Our place kickers practice daily in the spring and fall. It is important that the holder and kicker work as a team, because they must develop the timing that is vital to success in this maneuver.

Fake kick formations

Any number of passes and runs can be executed from a regular punt formation. It is common practice for a team using the strategy of punting frequently on third down also to run from this formation. We have not done this to any great extent from regular punt formation because we will usually kick from a quick-kick formation on any down other than fourth. As a result, we have had great success with a series of runs and passes from this quick-kick formation and I would

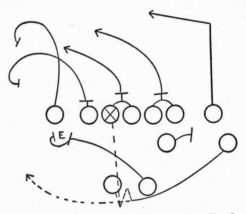

Fig. 109. The Fake Quick-Kick Handback.

like to diagram a series for you. If you have a left halfback who is adept at quick-kicking and you use this weapon frequently, I am sure that this fake quick-kick series will certainly increase his effectiveness.

First of all, there is the "fake quick-kick handback." The tailback goes through all of the motions of quick-kicking. Instead of kicking the ball he will hold it in his right hand behind his back and the right halfback will circle behind and take it out of his hand almost like a "Statue of Liberty." Everyone blocks just as if it is a quick-kick and then circles to the short side. The fullback invites the defensive end to the inside and tries to block him in (see Figure 109).

The next play that evolved in this series was the "quick-kick handback keep." On this play, the tailback fakes the quick-kick but holds the ball behind

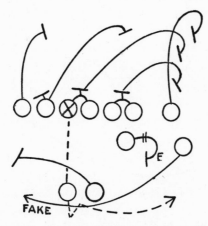

Fig. 110.   The Quick-Kick Handback Keep.

himself in his right hand. The right halfback circles behind and fakes as though he is taking the ball from the tailback. After holding this position long enough to let the defense be drawn by the fake of the right halfback, the tailback runs around the right flank. Once again, everyone blocks as if it is a quick-kick, only this time they will circle to the right. The quarterback will invite the end on that side to the inside and then will attempt to block him in (see Figure 110).

We have two passes that we use from the fake quick-kick series. The first is the "quick-kick handback pass" where everything is executed the same as in the "quick-kick handback," with the right halfback taking the ball from behind the back of the left halfback,

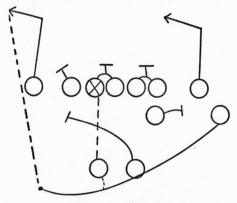

Fig. 111.   The Quick-Kick Handback Pass.

going around the left flank, and then stopping and passing to one of the ends downfield. These ends start down as though they were covering a kick and then break to the left (see Figure 111). We also execute a "quick-kick handback keep pass" where the tailback will fake the handback to the right halfback and will keep the ball. Then he passes to one of his ends who starts downfield with the ball and breaks to the right (see Figure 112).

184

When a team has used the field goal successfully, a fake field goal and run is often very effective. In our favorite fake field goal the holder will raise his knee as he catches the ball and allow the place kicker to go

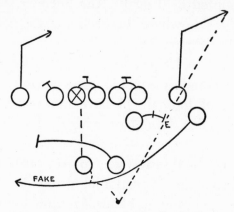

Fig. 112.   The Quick-Kick Handback Keep Pass.

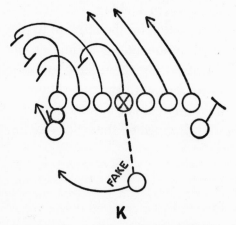

Fig. 113.   A Fake Field Goal Play.

through the motion of kicking the ball but miss it. The holder picks it up and carries it around one of the flanks, hoping to catch the defensive end on that side coming to the inside and trying to block what he thinks is an attempted field goal. The linemen once again circle to the side where the back is attempting to run the ball (see Figure 113).

In conclusion, I would like to reiterate that the kicking game is certainly equal in importance to any other department of football. I have never seen a great football team that didn't have a highly developed kicking game.

The easiest and fastest way to gain yardage is from an open formation. Spend a lot of time in perfecting precision-timed punt and kickoff returns because they will reap big dividends.

Our philosophy in kicking, whether it be a punt or a kickoff, is founded on the attempt to place the ball as close to our opponent's goal line as possible, not with the idea of letting them have an opportunity to score against us, but with the one thought in mind of gaining possession again at a point closer to their goal than when we relinquished the ball by kicking.

9

Organization

The most enjoyable hours the football coach spends in his profession are on the practice field with his players, and I think all coaches are greatly concerned about a way to get across the maximum enjoyment, along with knowledge, to their men.

Therefore, I believe the very first requirement should be that all coaches have an outline covering what they are going to do with each group on the field, and that the outline not permit them to stick at one thing too long. In other words, I do not think that it is a good thing to drill any one phase of the game over a half hour, or so. We try to change activities as often as every fifteen minutes.

To my way of thinking, a practice schedule should be set up from day to day and not too long in advance, because it is pretty hard to determine the progress made by your team. Consequently, your practice schedule must be flexible. The over-all practice schedule should be set up into two groups:

1. Group work
2. Team work where the team is working as a unit either offensively or defensively.

In group work it is well to spend your time on fundamentals, taking plays apart, or stressing specialties pertaining to the game of football. In your team work you develop your offensive timing. Your plays are given running and passing, and defenses are correlated.

Practice sessions can be too long and drawn out, and if this happens you will lose the interest of your players. I have known some of them to become fed up with football before the season ends. A player gets tired of working against his own teammates and may even stop looking forward to the games. I find that once the game is started, it is not too difficult to hold their attention.

Coaching is like teaching a class. You must have the students' attention and avoid detractions in order to get your points across. The players must take their examinations on Saturday in front of thousands of people, and now, with television in our midst, I might say millions. Therefore, we must prepare them so that they make a minimum of mistakes.

Staff organization is a very important part of coaching. In our meetings each man on the staff can express his opinion both for or against a subject, but, once we come out of the room and have made a decision, everyone must stick by it and not make remarks to the contrary.

I have heard assistant coaches say that if the team had only followed their suggestions as to defense, the game might have been won. The assistant coaches also have been known to second guess the head coach's judgment down on the field. I would say that this is not fair for an assistant coach to do because there may be a great number of circumstances down on the bench that he does not understand or that he knows nothing about.

If you win, there is glory for everyone, and if you

lose, there is glory for no one; therefore, each coach must add everything he can to the ultimate objective, which is to try to win the game.

Every coach has had many experiences, so, his judgment and recommendations should be given a good bit of consideration. Once a decision is made, then all should be for it. On the field one coach should not criticize another, and it has been the policy for all coaches not to have any disagreements in front of the players. If anything is to be said, it should be discussed in our own private meetings.

We all preach the importance of unity to our players; consequently, the staff should not only *preach* unity but *live* by it. An assistant coach should always keep in mind that he will be as successful as the head coach, just as the head coach will be as successful as his assistants.

A staff meeting should be held in a quiet place where it is impossible for anyone to break it up, except in case of an emergency. It should be set up with blackboards, a movie projector, and a screen.

As for field organization, all coaches at Michigan State have some classes. However, these classes are arranged so that each coach can report on the field a half-hour ahead of the regular practice schedule time. Thus, if any of the boys appear early, the coaches will be able to give instruction on individual specialties. I don't believe there is ever an excuse for a coach being late for his own practice.

At the time regularly scheduled for the players to appear, the head coach will blow his whistle, calling all men to the center of the field. There he will give out instructions and announcements, or he can start immediately on a fast calisthentics drill, grass drill, or some sort of warmup. After the warmup, the head coach can give new offensive plays, defensive set-ups or he can send his squad into group work immediately.

The line coach, end coach, and backfield coach will have charge of their own group and they can divide it up any way they see fit. In other words, if Steve Sebo, our backfield coach, wants to have some of the backs work on pass defense, he can take charge of that phase of the game and let the men who are assisting him be in charge of the offensive backs. There were times in the past three years when I was asked to take over the offensive backs, which I did, and the same holds true with the line.

Duffy Daugherty is in charge of the line and can make assignments and ask for any help necessary. John Kobs and Don Mason give Duffy a great deal of assistance in working with offensive and defensive line set-ups.

The ends are the responsibility of Earle Edwards, and he arranges for his own program, which would be

191

composed of fundamentals, pass catching drills, pass patterns, and defensive set-ups.

The thing I am trying to point out is that each assistant coach will have charge of his own department when group work is on. When the team drills start, the head coach has full responsibility and will make assignments to the others, depending on whether he is working on offense or defense.

At the end of practice it is a good thing to end up with a drill to help create unity and to act as a conditioner. We go so far as to have relays sometimes, with the ends, backs, and line all competing against one another. We practice the punting game, sprints, and signal drill, or we will block the dummies for a short period of time with most of the emphasis on speed and spirit.

As a member of the Big Ten, Michigan State is limited to a two-hour session each day, but this time is rarely ever used up. When the season gets under way those who play in the game are allowed to dress in sweat suits on Monday, and after a fast warmup they see movies of the previous game. Tuesday and Wednesday are the days for real work, but we never practice over an hour and fifteen minutes on Thursday. If we go over a half-hour on Friday, it is unusual. I have always had the motto of "Sacrificing almost everything for freshness," but, of course, discipline should never be sacrificed.

I think it would be well at this time to give you a sample practice schedule.

SAMPLE PRACTICE SCHEDULE

4:00 P.M. Head Coach calls squad together and gives them any announcements or comments. Have the squad take some fast calisthenics or run a couple of laps to warm up, then the coach will add plays or any special review that is necessary.

Team breaks up into group work for ends, backs, linemen. In group work the coaches analyze the offense and defense separately and work on the parts that make it go or fail. For example:

Line Offense—Daugherty, Line Coach

Work on 4-block and 5-block; be sure of getting the line blockers. Work on check blocks, preventing linemen from sliding to play. Work on pulling and heading up field instead of running the backs to the sidelines.

Line Defense—Kobs

Work on ball reaction, hitting the

dummy and going to the cutoff. Work on form tackling, keeping the head up. Work on position in various defenses.

Backs—Sebo (Offense)
All backs work with the centers on ball-handling and reviewing plays. Set up dummies and have backs work on hitting their holes. During this drill put emphasis on clutching the ball when hit.

Backs—(Defense) Devine
Work against a passing team, emphasizing normal coverage and playing the ball.
Pass-defense drill will stress all defensive men playing the ball.

Team Work

"A" Group

Teams 1 and 2 will go with Munn and Edwards.
These teams will work on offense against the dummies. It will be shifted to various defenses. This will be a hard review that pays particular attention to downfield blocking.

"B" Group   Teams 3 and 4 will work on defense under Daugherty and Sebo. This group will work on all rules of defense and will work hard to correlate the defensive backs with the line. This time put in rules of defense and practice position play. At the middle of the time allotted for this team work, I will switch groups. We will then practice with the punting drill and springs by position.

Quarterback strategy

There are three things that everybody can do better than anybody else:

1. Build a fire
2. Run a hotel
3. Quarterback a football team.

I am sure that the average fan has a peculiar conception of what constitutes a smart quarterback. In the final analysis, the success or failure of a play is their criterion for judgment. A typical remark is, "You are a smart quarterback if the play works; if it fails, you are lousy." Most football fans feel that a smart field general is one who mixes up his plays. He runs off tackle, he hits the line, he passes, and he kicks. "A smart quarterback," they say, "is one who had the defense guessing and tried them out in every spot." As a matter of fact, this orthodox conception of signal calling is far removed from the truth.

To be a good quarterback a boy must have several qualities:

1. He must have the personality to inspire the confidence of his teammates.
2. He must have a fine knowledge of the technique of football. This includes his own team as well as his opponent.
3. He must be able to co-ordinate all factors and have good judgment as far as calling plays is concerned.

A smart, capable quarterback is the greatest single asset that a team can have. A team can have a beautiful offense, but without anyone to call it, they are sunk. In other words, the quarterback is the pilot of the ship and he must steer that ship toward the goal line. A quarterback must be a planner and a thinker. When he is on defense he is thinking and planning his attack. During the time he is on offense he is putting these thoughts into reality and he must always remember what has been going on. Last, he must have the necessary offensive and defensive abilities to play his own position well. Some of his most important requirements are:

1. He must be a good blocker, capable of carrying out his assignment on every play. If he cannot carry his share of the offensive load he will lose "caste" with his teammates. He cannot expect them to do things that he cannot or will not do himself.

2. He must be a good tackler and be able to handle his share of the defense along with the rest of the team.

3. He must be a good pass defender. In this department of play, as well as on offense, he should be able to direct the play of his team and meet changing situations as they develop.

4. He must be a good ball handler. He should be able to finesse and carry out the deception that is so necessary to a well rounded offense.

5. He must have cadence, rhythm, and a voice that is understandable and has a *lift* to it. He sets the speed of play, the speed of the shift, and keeps the mental tone of the team at the pace he sets. If his voice drags, it will depress his team; but if he barks his sig-

nals clearly and with confidence, his team will rise up with the *rhythm* and *lift* of his voice.

A quarterback must have a fine knowledge of his plays. This involves:

A. Knowing each man's assignment on each play against every conceivable type of defense.
  1. It is impossible to call plays intelligently without knowing who blocks the various defensive men. If the defensive tackle is playing too wide but is not charging, the quarterback must know who will be blocking him and use the play to best take advantage of this defensive lapse. Just running inside of tackle is not enough; the quarterback, to best take advantage of the way the tackle is playing, must go inside of him *with the proper block.*
B. Each play being evaluated as to the results likely to be gained from running it. Plays can be classified roughly into four groups:
  1. Straight-ahead power plays that have very little chance of kicking back on you, with a small gain practically assured, but with a very small chance of a breakaway.
  2. Wide plays that have a possibility of gaining

a lot of yardage on one play, but that also may lose quite a bit. In other words, the quarterback is shooting for about a six-yard gain as against the chances of a loss. There is not much chance of making a yard or two, only.

3. Deceptive plays with the opportunity of gaining a great deal of yardage, but that also have the chance of kicking back on you for a big loss or a possible fumble.

4. Passes, laterals, or other such plays that have the chance of going for a long gain, but that have the possibility of interception, loss of ball, or a long yardage loss.

A quarterback must be able to execute properly all assignments himself if he expects teammates to follow. This gives him the confidence of his fellow players, and they look to such a leader. Football players will follow a leader who *leads* much more quickly than one who *tells*. There *is* a difference, so the quarterback should be sure that he carries out his own part on each assignment given him, no matter how mechanical it may be.

A quarterback should never gripe about a teammate or cause members of his team to complain about each other. Keeping his team well poised and emotionally smooth is part of his job. The coach will take

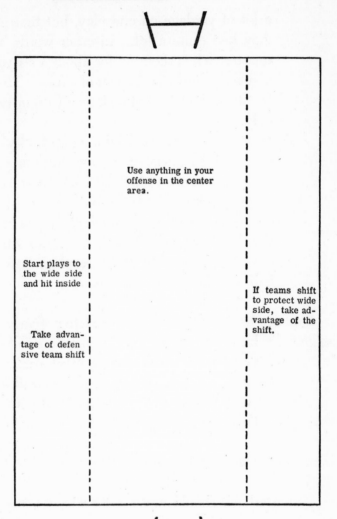

Use anything in your offense in the center area.

Start plays to the wide side and hit inside

Take advantage of defensive team shift

If teams shift to protect wide side, take advantage of the shift.

Fig. 114. Field-Position, Chart 1.

Zone of intense resistance

(1) Stick to plays that have worked
(2) Eliminate multiple ball handling plays
(3) Team must have poise and "cash in"
    their motto

—20

Best position for scoring plays
Start speeding up your attack
Any type of play should go & use lots of deception

—50

Between 35 and 40 kick 4th down
As you get near the center of field start working series
Ball handling plays can be used
Knock out the first downs

—20

Play for long gains
Pass long
Quick kick
Screen passes
Be sure of punt protection

Fig. 115.   Field-Position, Chart 2.

the responsibility for "pep" talks. The quarterback's responsibility is to carry out his own assignment efficiently and direct the offensive assignments of his teammates so that they will achieve maximum results.

A quarterback must have the ability to spot defensive weaknesses and take advantage of what the other team is doing. Each coach has many different ways of teaching his quarterbacks, so, to avoid confusion, I am just going to try to give some general principles on the subject.

A quarterback must know all of the conditions of the game. These include every phase of the weather, position on the field, score of the game, time to be played, yardage, the type of defense the opponents are playing, the capabilities of all men on his own team, what they have done to affect the defense, and so on. We will discuss two of these a little further:

> 1. *Weather conditions.* If you are going *against* the wind, run the plays a little more slowly. On a windy day short hook passes are better than long ones because the ball is easier to control. If the day is wet, plays that have less ball-handling are better to use. If you are going *with* the wind, use the quick-kick, run your plays faster, pass longer, and, of course, use the punt.

2. *Position on the field.* The field is divided into sections; the yardage strips are regular divisions. You should always know where you are from a longitudinal stand and your field is automatically divided laterally with the ball being moved in approximately 17 yards. In former years, the position on the field meant more than it does today, and I have seen some of the best teams in college football throw passes when they were on their own one-yard line. In my days of playing football, 22 years ago, the game was more conservative, and today the offenses have advanced tremendously over that era. To illustrate, I am going to draw up two charts on field position (see Figures 114 and 115).

It is my personal opinion that a quarterback is evaluated on how well he controls his team and on how well he gets the ball over the goal line. Actually, he is judged just as a team is—does he win or does he lose? I have seen a team gain over 400 yards on a field and have the opposing team gain 61, but the latter group kicked the try-for-point and won the game 7-6.

I would get into quite a controversy if I named the best quarterback I have had, but one of the finest was quite a controversial figure with the fans. He ended up by winning a tremendous number of games.

A complete book in itself could be written on quarterback strategy, but I do hope the points I have mentioned will be worthwhile.

Index

Index